CW00641785

Working with Gun Dogs

Working with Gun Dogs

Hunter Adair

ROBERT HALE · LONDON

© Hunter Adair 2006
First published in Great Britain 2006

ISBN-10: 0-7090-8054-9
ISBN-13: 978-0-7090-8054-1

Robert Hale Limited
Clerkenwell House
Clerkenwell Green
London EC1R 0HT

The right of Hunter Adair to be identified as
author of this work has been asserted by him
in accordance with the Copyright, Designs
and Patents Act 1988.

A catalogue record for this book is available from
the British Library

2 4 6 8 10 9 7 5 3 1

Typeset in 10/13½pt Sabon
by e-type, Liverpool
Printed in Great Britain by Gomer Press Limited

Contents

Illustrations

13 Game shooters with their dogs on a crisp, frosty morning in Northumberland

14 A spaniel guarding the pheasants in the boot of an estate car in the farmyard

15 Two working sheepdogs housed by the roadside on the moors

16 Bill and Pat Colclough. Bill is a gamekeeper on Blanchland Moor in Co. Durham

17 Wenty Beaumont, with his dog, Oscar, at Bywell, near Stocksfield, Northumberland

18 An adder sunning itself out on the moors

19 A cock pheasant with a plastic clip on its beak which stops the bird from feather pecking and causes no discomfort

20 The author, Hunter Adair, at home with his springer spaniel called Percy at the end of a pheasant shoot

Between pages 88 and 89

21 Standing guns at a pheasant shoot waiting for the pheasants being flushed over them

22 The game shooters returning from a pheasant drive at lunchtime near the Scottish border

23 The woodcock is a mysterious little bird and has been hunted for centuries by man

24 The author on his farm at Hexham in Northumberland

25 Dog with a mallard duck. The author often uses a mallard duck for dog training sessions

26 This particular dog was an excellent gun dog and extremely intelligent

27 Two gamekeepers on a shoot in the north

28 The kestrel is a lovely bird of prey which is also known as the windhover due to its habit of hanging motionless in the air

All illustrations are from the author's collection.

Introduction

We are a nation of dog lovers, and there are over four million dogs in this country. Yet many of their owners overfeed them and fail to give them sufficient exercise to keep them fit and in good health.

Poor management can lead to all sorts of problems for many dogs. They can develop kidney trouble and arthritis, to name just two diseases, and this can shorten the animal's life by two or three years.

Sportsmen who work with dogs in the field will not get the best out of their animals if they are overweight. Before the end of the day's work outside, many dogs have slowed down so much that they almost have to be carried home.

Innumerable dogs also lack proper training and seem to run wild when they are out in the field. I see a lot of gun dogs being worked, and running about chasing everything that moves for their own pleasure, rather than being kept under their handler's control.

I have been working and training dogs since I was about seven years old, and have studied the behaviour and temperament of many breeds. Accordingly I hope that the knowledge and experience I have gained and recorded in this book will prove of assistance to other owners in the

constant search for a harmonious and effective partner-
ship with their dogs.

1

Choosing a Dog

When it comes to selecting a dog, most people have their own preference for certain breeds. Some sportsmen like smaller dogs – for example, springer spaniels – but one of the most popular breeds is the labrador, for these make very good working gun dogs, as well as delightful family pets.

There are many different strains and breeds of labrador and spaniel around. Some are bred with big bones and broad heads, others with short legs and fine bones. Certain breeders are well known for the type and strain they produce, and when you see some gun dogs working, they may have certain characteristics which can help you to recognize the breeder or kennels from which that particular dog originates.

It is very difficult to advise anyone on which breed of dog they should buy, because there are so many important points that should be considered before going ahead and buying a young puppy. First of all, why does the purchaser want the dog? Is he or she going to train it to work as a gun dog, is it to be used for exhibitions, or is it just wanted as a family pet because the prospective owner is attracted to a certain breed of animal? And there are many other factors to take into account as well: for example, where is it going to be kept, and who is going to look after it?

Over the past fifty years or so, many people's housing accommodation has changed. In the cities, most rows of back-to-back houses have been knocked down, and many of the tenants rehoused in multi-storey blocks of flats. Although many back-to-back houses had no gardens, a lot of the residents could, and did, keep all the various types of pets, including dogs of all sorts, and many of these people enjoyed the pleasure of hunting with their dogs. (Some of them, however, disregarded the countryside rules, and did a bit of poaching with their whippets, grey-hounds and lurchers.)

There is no reason why an owner cannot have a dog which takes them to shows and exhibitions, as well as being useful as a top-class working dog. In practice, though, such dual-purpose animals are very few and far between, as training a dog for the show bench is completely different from training one for working with fur and feather in the field.

There are many breeds and strains of spaniel. Some breeders have greatly improved the spaniel as a working dog, although some are no longer fit to work in the field – in fact various strains which appear on the show bench are only able to walk around the show ring a few times before they are exhausted. The spaniel breed in general, however, is in pretty good shape and one must remember it is only those from a few selected strains which are unsuitable as gun dogs; the majority are quite fit for field work. Some of the judges of sporting gun dogs are, in many cases, sportsmen themselves, and may judge the animal from a working point of view.

If you get a chance to go along to a dog show or exhibition, it will be time well spent looking at the various breeds of dogs, and you might be able to see which type or breed of dog will suit your needs. Whether you want one as a pet, or as a working gun dog, the different varieties are all most likely to be there, and you will see dogs of all shapes and sizes. And should you attend some gun dog trials or a dog show and want advice about a particular breed, then look around and you may see a gamekeeper or breeder who, I am sure, would be very willing to help and advise you all they can. Gamekeepers in general have plenty of experience with working gun dogs, and they would help you to select an animal that will at least have the appearance of a good working dog, and it probably will be a good dog. Some gamekeepers breed gun dogs, and are well known amongst the shooting fraternity for the type of working dogs they breed. Once you have in mind the type and breed you want, it is worthwhile looking around and getting advice about that strain of dog.

Most breeders of sporting dogs will also be very pleased to see anyone at their kennels who is interested in purchasing one of their animals. There are many good breeders of working gun dogs in this country, who have a lot of experience, and if you have any doubts about selecting a dog, consult the owner of the kennels, who will have the knowledge and will advise you on some of the good points and bad points to look for in a dog. Advice of this kind will be very useful and helpful when you come to selecting a puppy from a litter on your own. Someone else's expertise can be invaluable. Before you buy one, you will know how big the dog will eventually grow, and how much space, accommodation, and food it will eventually need.

It is unwise to think that all labradors, spaniels, setters and pointers, etc., are good working gun dogs. This is far from the truth, as many examples of these breeds will be useless when it comes to working in the field, even if the dogs have pedigrees as long as your arm. The breeding of animals of various kinds is a very skilled job indeed. Many dairy farmers will tell you it can take a lifetime to breed dairy cows that have good conformation and good udders, have high yields, and produce high-quality milk. There are many farmers who breed top-quality pedigree cattle in this country, as well as those who breed top-quality cattle which are not pedigree. The latter probably get more money for their stock when they sell them.

When artificial insemination of cattle was introduced in this country in the early 1940s, the improvement in the quality was tremendous, especially among the many small farms in the Dales. However, there has been no such large-scale improvement in sporting dogs generally, although some really good breeders have improved the quality of some particular breeds of sporting dog over the last thirty or forty years.

Some people have a good eye when it comes to selecting a dog, horse, sheep or cow, without ever knowing if the animal is from pedigree stock or not, and in most cases they are never very far wrong. I know a few people among the farming community who are well known for being able to select good-quality stock even from day-old calves. The same applies among our canine friends; some people can just look at a dog and tell you if it is any good, even if they have never seen it before. This is a gift that some have, and I see this more in the farming world. The few people who can tell you if a young puppy will make a good gun dog and work well in the field are very rare. They are born with this gift and not made.

The plainest-looking sporting dog will probably have some interesting features which may attract the average sportsman; it may have a friendly face, attractive eyes, or a good colour. Although some sportsmen may think that because a gun dog is plain looking, it will not be good at field work, this is not necessarily the case – it may turn out to be the most obedient working dog around. The point here is, never think that because a dog is plain looking, it is no good at working in the field. I see all types and breeds of working dogs, and sometimes I see the scruffiest-looking animal working away, doing a first-class job, despite the fact that it is cross-bred. The dog has learnt the necessary skills from the trainer and is putting them into practice.

SELECTING AND CARING FOR A PUPPY

When it comes to selecting or buying a puppy, there is one thing that should be considered long before finally deciding what breed or size of dog to purchase. Many people buy a puppy for their sons or daughters as a Christmas or birthday present, and they forget that a young puppy takes a lot of looking after all the time. They also don't always take into consideration that the puppy will grow up to be a big dog, and that it will need a lot of attention every day. It will need to be fed, watered and exercised regularly. People often buy a large breed of dog when their accommodation is inadequate for dogs of any sort. A young puppy looks very attractive and cuddly, and so people frequently buy one for the wrong reason. The result is that, after a few weeks, the puppy becomes a nuisance to the parents, and the children lose all interest in it, because it starts chewing everything in the house due to boredom.

The parents then get fed up with the dog and kick it out onto the street. If they had initially sought advice about the dog, the attention that the animal would need and the amount of time involved in looking after it properly, they would have thought twice about buying their offspring a puppy.

Stray dogs are a widespread problem in this country, and many councils now employ dog-catchers or wardens. People who are fed up with their puppies or dogs should contact a dog shelter, who I am sure will take the animals off their hands and try to find a good home for them, rather than boot them out onto the streets, where they can become a nuisance and a danger to traffic. And if dogs are left to run wild in the countryside, they are a menace among sheep and cattle. The dog shelters in this country do a great job (some are even open twenty-four hours a day) and will always be willing to give guidance and help to those wanting advice.

Most people who buy gun dogs to work, like myself, have the dog as a family friend as well as a working dog. Before I purchase one, the welfare and accommodation for the animal is discussed and thought out. Some people may like setter dogs very much, but may not have suitable housing for such a large animal, so they decide on a smaller breed, such as a spaniel or a labrador.

Very young puppies should never be allowed to run all over a house unsupervised. They should be confined to some corner of the house or kennel to start with. The pup should also have some material to play with and chew at, such as a small rubber or woollen ball, or an old shoe. Any type of material of this sort will be sufficient to keep it amused when it is not being attended to.

Small puppies will wet and mess all over the house if they are not confined and supervised at least until they are house trained. This can take anything from two to six weeks, depending on how much time is spent with the animal. It should be taken outside after each small meal or drink. There is no need to leave a dish with water or milk in it all the time, as this encourages the puppy to drink and wet every half hour or so. The puppy should be given a drink when fed and then the dish should be removed until it is fed again.

After young pups have been weaned, they should be fed three or four times a day for several weeks. They should eat their food quickly, then the dish should be taken from them until the next feeding time. By the time the dog is about one year old, it should be on one feed a day, preferably in the evening and at regular times. A dog should gulp its food in a few minutes.

When a dog lives in the house, and comes in from the field, or after being exercised on a wet muddy day, make sure that it is cleaned. A smaller animal, of course, takes less cleaning, and makes less of a mess of your home than a large, wet dog would do. After being in the field, always give the dog a good rub down with an old towel or cloth, and keep it away from heat when it's wet, so that it can dry naturally.

My preference is for small working dogs, such as the smaller strains of spaniel or labrador. I take time to hunt for a small type of either breed, and at the same time I look for a dog with a good pedigree involving dogs with a working track record. These qualities satisfy me that at least I have the foundation for a good working dog, and I have never had a dog that was really useless. All the gun dogs I have worked with have had a variety of qualities amongst them; some were very placid with a good nature, others would bite children if they were allowed to. (A word about dogs that bite. There are usually one or two reasons for this happening, the main one being that the dog hasn't got room to escape, so it attacks you. A dog which is tied up may bark at you, and if you go too close it will probably attack and bite you, feeling hemmed in. It doesn't *want* to bite you, and if it can get out of your road, it will. Most wild animals behave in this way; they stay away from people, and it's only when people get so close that the animal can't escape, that it will then feel trapped and attack.)

MAKING THAT IMPORTANT FINAL CHOICE

When you have decided on the breed and type of gun dog you require, the day will come when you go to select a puppy from a breeder. Whether you intend training the dog yourself, or having the dog trained for you to work in the field, there are a few points to look for in a puppy which may help you make the right choice.

Remember you are looking for an animal that will be working for you over the next ten to fifteen years, so take your time, and don't let anyone distract you by saying that they like this or that puppy, because there may be a conflict of interests. If you happen to get the first pick of the litter, ask the breeder to let the puppies run loose in the garden or kennels, and study the action of all the pups. You will soon notice the puppies that are running around fully alert, chasing everything that moves. If there are one or two puppies in the litter full of go, then one of these is for you. You will also see puppies that are timid and retreat as soon as you move, looking for a corner to hide in. There is no doubt which of these pups will make the best gun dog: the bold ones with the strong temperaments. But they will also take some handling. What a tremendous challenge to a sportsman, though, training such a bold animal!

Now that you have eliminated the timid dogs, have a closer look at the ones which show the most promise. Sort out the ones you like for colour. Of course, if they are all the same shade, this problem is solved, but if they are a litter of spaniels, they are sure to all have different markings. Sort out two with markings and colour you fancy. Then examine the pups in fairly close detail for conformation, and, provided they are in good health, then one of them is for you.

The dog's feet are very important, as it has to put in a full day's work in the field. It should have suitably sized feet which are close and compact; they should be straight, not spreading or splayed. No matter how good-looking it is, if its feet are not right, pass the dog over.

Most good working gun dogs should have dark eyes; dogs with light coloured or small, sunken eyes are normally unpredictable, and sometimes erratic in their behaviour. Most judges in the show ring will pass over a dog with very light-coloured or small eyes, for these tell you a great deal about the animal's character. Some gun dogs use their eyes as much as their nose when hunting. Some sportsmen say that the dog should not work the ground too close with its nose, but should keep looking up and around to see where its master is when it is hunting and working at full stretch.

A working gun dog should have a nice round head. There is a tendency with some breeds to have long narrow heads, and a rounded head at least tells you that the dog should have some brains. The jaws and mouth should be level, and dogs with an undershot jaw won't be much good at retrieving game. Its muzzle should be a good size, with clear open nostrils, which are ideal for finding game on a bad scenting day. Dogs with very short muzzles may find it difficult to retrieve large game, such as hares, and will grip the game hard and mark it. You will receive a lower price for damaged game from the dealer.

The conformation of a working dog is very important. It should have a good length of neck in proportion to its body, for carriage. It should also have strong muscular thighs and a fairly deep chest, to give pace and staying power. A dog with all these qualities will be able to work his heart out all day on a grouse moor, or flushing pheasants from woods, coverts or plantations.

Sam Gibson and his father, Derwent, who owns Embley Farm and the shoot in Hexham – with friends Bill Bailey and the author (*far right*). The author has been shooting at Embley Farm for over 30 years

The author working his gun dog on a Durham grouse moor trying to find shot grouse

A shooting party at
Embley Farm, Hexham

The author at home training
a dog with game birds

A young cocker spaniel
is being encouraged to
bring a pheasant to his
master

A group of game shooters at Wall in Northumberland

Pheasant shooters at the end of a drive with their dogs, near Carlisle

The international pointer and setter gun dog trials being held on Blanchland Moor in Co. Durham

Most golden retrievers are bouncy, playful dogs and generally have a good temperament

This is a wood where the author often walks his gun dogs and where he meets people with various breeds of dog

I have already remarked on the things one should think about before considering having a dog of any sort, the suitability of your house being most important (flats pose difficulties for any animal). Plenty of time must be available, too, for looking after your animal. However, whatever you choose, if you choose well, with the help of the above points, you should get a better-than-average dog.

I see all breeds of dogs working in the field amongst game birds, and the best are not always pedigree. Some cross-bred dogs work away all day flushing game birds, doing a first-class job for their owners. However, if you are intending to start from scratch and are wanting a gun dog, get the best breed you can afford from a strain with a good track record. You should then have a dog that will give you plenty of confidence with which to start working.

BOARDING KENNELS

If you own a dog, be prepared to give a good part of your life to its needs; but in return, what a great amount of pleasure and companionship you will get from your canine friend! Dogs do need a lot of care and attention. If you go on holiday, you have to think what to do with your pet. Do you leave it with some friends, or put it into boarding kennels, or do you take it on holiday with you? You have to make plans well ahead when you are thinking about leaving home for a few days.

There are some very good kennels around; I use some from time to time and find them excellent. If your dog has a bed or basket at home, take this with you when it goes into kennels, or take its blanket or towel – something which the dog lies on or plays with. It will then know that you are coming back for it. I know that most kennels do provide bedding, but it can be quite stressful for your animal to be taken from its home and put in amongst strangers. Its favourite toys will be a great comfort to it, and it will not feel that it is being left. Once the dog has been in the kennels a few times with its own gear, this will make it easier, although it may not be too chuffed at being taken from its home!

2

The General Training
of Gun Dogs

There are many points of view on the pros and cons of
when to start training a young puppy, and how to
teach it discipline. Over the past sixty-odd years, I have
been training and working with gun dogs, mainly labradors
and springer spaniels, and I strongly believe that although
one can try to explain the basis of how to discipline a dog,
the best knowledge is obtained by doing the job oneself.

Sometimes I see setters or pointers out working in the
field, but, in general, labradors and spaniels seem to be the
most commonly used gun dogs. Remember, however, that
most breeds of dog are in origin working breeds: lurchers,
terriers and sheep dogs, to name just a few. Professional gun
dog trainers will have coached many dogs through their
hands, and will have learnt a great deal about the behaviour
and peculiarities of the various breeds. They will also have
a tremendous knowledge of the techniques involved, built
up over the years. Some of these people discipline their dogs
to a very high standard, producing even field trial cham-
pions. There are also many thousands of amateur gun dog
trainers in this country, amongst whom I put myself, and

there is no reason why non-professionals cannot train their dogs to a fairly high standard. (When discussing amateur trainers, I am talking about the thousands of people who either lease a small shoot, or are part of a shooting syndicate, and prefer to train their own animals to work with them in the field.) There are also many people living in towns and cities who own gun dogs which they may not use

for shooting. These are usually labradors, retrievers or springer spaniels, and they keep them as family pets. And why not? They can be well-trained loving animals.

Most sportsmen who own gun dogs get a great deal of pleasure by working with their dogs in the field. On a crisp, frosty morning, there is nothing better than walking a rough shoot with a few friends and their animals, and seeing well-trained gun dogs working is very pleasing. Unfortunately, however, a great many are very poorly drilled. One or two ill-disciplined dogs running about on a shooting day, chasing everything that moves can spoil the sport for others. On countless occasions whilst out in the field, I, and many others, have overheard someone saying, 'I wish somebody would shoot that ****** dog or put it on a lead!' This situation often arises when either one of the shooters or a beater has a dog that runs about at will, uncontrolled. The owner spends most of the day bawling and shouting at his animal, which really is a hindrance rather than a help. The dog should be left at home until it has some further training. It is difficult to do anything about this, for if it is the shoot-owner's dog, little can be said in case one doesn't get invited back to his shoot! I have often seen the shoot-owner's dogs hunting away too far in front of the beaters, and the owner bawling and cursing at them, while the dogs were taking no notice of him whatsoever. Some days this has been quite embarrassing!

I would think that, of all the gun dogs I see working the field, only about one in five is anything like being trained – although many I see have some good qualities, if only their owners were able to exploit these and get the best from their dogs. Many are spoiled partly because they are not given enough regular training, as their owners don't know how to do this adequately. They spend insufficient time with their animals each day. Even when the dog is being exercised, some of this time should be used for their education.

Training gun dogs is not easy, although some breeds are easier to discipline than others. Labradors in general need less schooling. A gamekeeper friend of mine, who has trained over a hundred gun dogs, once said that one should train labradors for several years before tackling springer spaniels. This is sound advice. To train a male springer spaniel with a strong temperament to a very high standard, as an obedient working gun dog in the field in all conditions, is quite a challenge, so it is preferable to have some practical experience with a less-demanding breed first.

The reason why so many dogs are badly trained is because their owners need training first. This includes the owners of family pets as well as sportsmen who buy gun dogs to work in the field. Some sportsmen pay a lot of money for a gun dog, expecting that because the animal is from a good working strain, it should automatically hunt, retrieve, go into water, stop, sit and not chase game. However, this will not happen without a great deal of discipline. All breeds, labradors, spaniels, pointers, setters and retrievers are bred to hunt, and they will run on and chase game for miles for their own pleasure, if they are not given some initial obedience training. No matter how intelligent it is, some fundamental training is necessary, even if the animal is not being used for work and is only a family pet. Otherwise, it can often become a nuisance both to the owners and to their neighbours. If the dog is to be used among fur and feather, the more regular and correct training it is given, the more useful it will be to its owner, who will also receive much pleasure from seeing his dog working well in the field.

If a hunting dog doesn't have the natural instinct to pursue game, it won't make a good working dog. It may, however, make a super pet, and there is nothing wrong with that. A suitable dog should not need to be trained to hunt – it should do this naturally on its own, and always be raring to go. Training the dog should involve disciplining it to hunt within a certain range – about thirty metres in front of the owner and thirty metres on either side – and to quarter the ground. Inside this area, the animal has to learn its craft. This includes learning to stop hunting when asked, to keep looking round when hunting to see where its trainer is, and not to get too far in front. The most important thing is to keep the dog within this hunting range. Within this compass, the animal has to learn to sit and come to heel when asked. It shouldn't need teaching how to retrieve game birds, for this should come naturally to it and be bred into it. However, its retrieving skills can be polished a great deal – again, all within this thirty-metre range.

The trainer needs to know exactly what he expects of his dog in the field, so that he can confidently teach his animal, for the dog has to learn its skills as an apprentice. I try to think myself into the animal's mind and attempt to make the dog consider what I am wanting it to do. This takes time, but if you persevere, the dog will eventually start responding to you. As it learns its skills within this hunting range, and you keep training, the dog will gradually get to know what is required, and this will help to polish its own hunting techniques. The more it works at its skills in the field, the better it will be at its job. This is certainly not a five-minute undertaking. In fact, far from it!

It may take years for a gun dog to become efficient at working and retrieving game in the field. This will depend a great deal on how much work the dog gets among the game birds, and how much training the owner puts into it. When the dog becomes good at working in the field, it won't forget the skills it has learnt from its trainer, but will build on them with its own skills. This is what makes a top-quality working gun dog, and it is priceless. Over the years I have had many good gun dogs, which I have trained myself. One particular springer spaniel was a real top-notch dog that turned out to be even better than I could have imagined. I was offered a blank cheque for him, but that dog wasn't for sale! When he learnt the skills I taught him, he then put his own skills into play, and what a brilliant animal he turned out to be. He used to use body language and eye contact with me to tell me if there were any game birds or hares lying ahead of us. When I read the signs from him, I used to tell my friends to look out, as there were game birds ahead of us. When the game was eventually flushed, some friends would ask how I knew that there were game birds lying ahead. When I said that the dog had told me, some of them told me not to be so ****** stupid: how could the dog tell me what was lying ahead! I said to them that he could – and he did!

One day some of my shooting friends were taught a lesson about how good this dog of mine was. Four of them

and I were walking across a rough field, shooting hares over our dogs. In the middle of the irregular field, there was a small clump of trees with long grass; they formed a shelter belt for the cattle in bad weather. As we approached this, my dog told me by his eyes and body language that there was no game in the small wood, and he wasn't going to bother hunting through it. As the dog and I walked round the outside of the copse, two of my friends suggested that I should put the dog in to hunt it out. When I commented that there was nothing there, they asked how I knew, so I replied that the dog had told me. I suggested that they both stood at the far end of the thicket, and I would get the dog to hunt it through to them. The dog didn't seem in the least interested, but went in and hunted through as ordered. Sure enough, there were no game birds hiding there. I asked my friends if they now believed me. They were astonished, and for the rest of that afternoon they wanted to know how my dog was communicating with me.

This dog and I have also arrived amongst game shooters, whose dogs were hunting for, and unable to find a pheasant that one of them said he had shot and that had dropped in a certain area. I would ask my dog to go and find the pheasant where the shooter thought it had fallen, and if the dog came back to me within a few minutes without the pheasant, I would be pretty sure it hadn't fallen to the ground in that area. Some game shooters sometimes think they have grounded a pheasant, when the bird is only gliding close to the ground, and hasn't been hit. I have many times hunted for a bird that is supposed to have been shot, and there have been no signs of the bird ever dropping to the ground.

Sometimes, game birds that have been shot at may look as if they are falling to the ground, when they are not. This depends a great deal on the type of land over which you are shooting. On hilly terrain it is sometimes very difficult to tell if a bird that has been shot at is falling to the ground or not.

———•◆•———

I have been involved with working dogs all my life, and have come across some great characters amongst them. However, you get the odd strange one. I can remember being given a young collie by a neighbour. We started the dog working amongst the sheep and cattle, and it began developing quite well. The collie had rather more white on it than I liked, and there was something about the animal that I couldn't figure out. It would never come to anybody to be stroked, or fussed with.

One day, this collie went missing, so the ploughman and I set out to search for it. We found it in the marsh field, worrying a sheep in a ditch, its face covered in blood. When it saw us, it showed its true character by turning, and baring its teeth at us. It was like a wild dog with its prey. The shotgun was brought, and the dog was shot at the scene. It was a danger to both people and animals alike!

3

The Initial Training of Gun Dogs

When one buys a gun dog puppy of about eight weeks old to train as a working dog, and the puppy is kept in the house with the family, then it is good advice to put a little collar on it and tie it up from time to time during the day, just for a few minutes. This gets the puppy used to a lead and to being led if you wish to take it into town, or out for a walk. Normally puppies don't like the infringement of their freedom involved in having a collar, or being tied up, but after a few days they soon get used to this, and it causes little distress to the animal.

If the puppy is housed in a kennel, then it doesn't need to be collared as quickly, because the kennel will have a wire netting run, and the puppy's movements will be fairly well restricted anyway. Animals kept in kennels normally don't come into contact with other dogs or people as much as puppies living in the house with the family.

TEN WEEKS

There are several points of view on when to start training a young gun dog. I have always started this as soon as the puppy has been weaned, when it is about ten weeks old. My dogs have always lived with the family. If the puppy is to live in the home, it first has to be house trained. When I take it into the garden to do its business, I use part of this exercise time to make the puppy sit once or twice. I then walk a few feet away from it, and if it moves towards me I take it back and start again. It takes weeks to master this, but keep at it. If, however, it is a very timid puppy, it will take longer. If the animal keeps coming amongst your feet, put his lead on, tie him to a post in the garden and make the puppy sit, then walk away from him a few feet. With time and patience, the puppy will soon get the message. This training must be done gently and slowly, for you won't gain anything by trying to rush it, and you will bore the young dog.

When the puppy is in the house with the family, I some-times tie a knot in a handkerchief and get it to make a few retrieves. This can also be done with a small rubber ball, or any other soft material, but again, two or three retrieves an evening is quite sufficient. This can be related to play with the dog, and so should not be rushed.

Where a puppy is kept in a kennel, there is no need to start as early with its training because kennel puppies have fewer distractions than a family pup, and are less likely to develop faults early on in their young lives. Also, many kennel dogs are not house trained and don't need to be, as they are normally never in their owner's home. A game-keeper may have his dogs out with him two or three times a day, and he can allow the animals more freedom and still have control over them, as he will use part of this time to train the dogs daily.

Many gamekeepers and country folk keep their gun dogs in a kennel, whereas those living in towns and cities (and there are many of them) may have no garden or backyard, so have to keep their dogs in the house. The latter may use their dogs for working in the field amongst fur and feather, and they often do a great job with their animals.

FIFTEEN WEEKS

As time passes, and the young dog reaches around fifteen weeks old, the trainer should be able to make it sit and then walk away from it for about twenty-five metres or so. Remember to keep this initial training within the shooting range, which is about thirty metres. Never send a young dog out to make a retrieve when it is sitting away out from the trainer; always call it to heel before sending it out.

At this stage a training dummy can be introduced to the young pup. A dried hare skin (which I use), a canvas dummy, or a stuffed nylon stocking are all ideal for this purpose. Make the dog sit and throw the dummy out over behind it, then walk away from the dog for several metres, and call it to heel before sending it out to retrieve the dummy. Again, at this training stage, two or three retrieves is plenty.

I like to use a dried hare skin for this type of training, as this is the dog's first introduction to game, and the animal will relate this to rabbits and hares, and therefore there will be less chance of it running in on them when they have been flushed. Any game dealer will dry a hare skin for you, or you can dry it yourself by just hanging it up in the garage or shed, and letting it desiccate. A hare skin can be obtained from a fishmonger that deals with game, or from a specialist game dealer. You could always shoot your own hare and skin it yourself, for it is not a difficult job and will only take a few weeks to dry out.

When the hare skin has dried, cut a piece of brush shaft and tie the pelt around it with a bit of string. It is very important here that you cut the piece of wood long enough, so that the dog has to pick it up by the middle and *not* by the end: it should be about 12–14 inches

(30–35 centimetres) in length. If it is much shorter, the dog will be inclined to pick the skin up by the end, and what you want it to do is to pick it up by the middle, as it would pick up a pheasant. If you have a small spaniel or labrador and the animal picks up the stick of this suggested length by the end, the hare skin will trail on the ground and the dog will drop it. It will then pick it up correctly by the middle. It is very important that a gun dog should retrieve game birds and hares by the body, so as not to damage them, and using dummies like this helps to drill it to do this.

Training gun dogs should be regular and in short sessions. You can't coach a dog just at the weekends and expect to have a really good, obedient dog. Short, regular training sessions are the best way to bring on a young dog. A big mistake that people make with a young gun dog, when exercising it in a lane, park or wood, is to let it run too far in front. As the dog is bred to hunt, this practice makes training more difficult. You should keep turning the dog back, and remember to keep it within a range of no more than thirty metres; it will have plenty of scope within that compass to play and exercise. In time, the dog will start looking round and turning back itself within this hunting range. This takes time, and you have to work at it with the dog. Some sportsmen with gun dogs have little time during the week with their dogs, so sometimes their wives or families have to take the animals out for their daily exercise. It is very important that they also know to keep turning the dog back whilst out walking it.

It is best to use a dog whistle when working a dog in the field, rather than bawling and shouting at it. There is nothing worse than shouting, for it disturbs the game for miles around, and in the shooting field the game birds will hear the culprit in the next county and scarper. Simple language should also be used when the dog is around you, to make it sit, or come to heel. I use a whistle when the dog is working out from me, and my voice when it is around my feet. I find this the best combination when training an animal. When using the whistle in the field, I give one peep to stop the dog, and two peeps to call it back to heel. If it is close at hand, I call it with my voice.

Many people training gun dogs go about it the wrong way. If a young dog likes water, or has a good nose, or retrieves well, they concentrate on these good points. However, all these can be developed later. But if you don't have full control of your dog by the time it is fifteen months old, then you will have a difficult job on your hands, especially if it is a strong-headed male dog. If you happen to buy a young gun dog that is about a year old, instead of a puppy, then start from the beginning with its training, and you can still knock the dog into shape and discipline it to a very high standard. However, you will have to spend more time with an older dog, as the animal will have picked up some faults by then. Some game-keepers don't start training their gun dogs until they are about fifteen months old, but remember that they may have their young dogs out with them two or three times a day, and this amount of time spent with the dogs will knock them into shape quicker. For most people with a full-time job, half an hour each day with their dogs may be all that is possible.

A YEAR TO FIFTEEN MONTHS

When the young gun dog reaches this age, it can be introduced to quartering the ground, whether it is a retriever, labrador or a spaniel. For this type of training, keep to ground where you can see the dog working all the time. A rough grass field or a small wood which is fairly open and clear at ground level, or out on the moors, is ideal country for this type of training. Start off by sending it out to your left for about twenty metres, then turn it either by whistle or voice and bring the dog back across your toes. Then send the dog out to the right and do the same. It is very important that you keep walking forward slowly as the dog is quartering the ground, and remember to keep it crossing right in front of you.

A long piece of string or thin rope can be used to help you start this type of training. It takes some time to get the dog quartering the ground properly, so keep changing the ground you work on so that it doesn't get bored. If you can use terrain where there are game birds about, the dog will be even more keen to get on with the job. (If you don't have such an area locally, then a gamekeeper or someone with a small shoot might let you use their ground in return for you and your dog helping them to beat on shooting days.) Once the dog gets to know when to turn as it quarters, then you have cracked it – however, it takes time and a lot of hard work to get to this stage. When you are training it to quarter the ground, it will be sure to flush game or a rabbit from time to time. Every time it does so, stop the dog and call it back to heel. Make a great fuss of it when it does it right. Also,

remember when using a dried hare skin on a training lesson, that the dog will relate this to the real thing when it is flushed, and the animal should immediately stop when asked to do so.

As the dog's training progresses, a shot or two can be fired over it. The best way to go about this is to get a friend, or someone with a shotgun, and ask them to stand about fifty metres away from the dog to start with, and then fire a shot. Watch to see how the dog reacts to this sudden noise. You can use a small starting pistol with blanks for this job, as long as you keep well away from the dog while you fire the shots around it. You will soon find out if it is gun-shy or not.

There are various places that you can go to with your young dog to improve its training. Visiting a grouse moor or a pheasant shoot in progress will be good experience. Remember to keep it on the lead and let it watch what is going on. Also, whilst training a young dog, take it out into the countryside among sheep and cattle – especially the former, because they are inclined to run when they see a dog. Make the dog sit when it sees the ewes and lambs run. If possible, walk through amongst them with the dog on the lead and keep making the dog sit as the animals run. In time, it will get to know not to chase them. You can let the dog off the lead once you are confident that you can stop it by using the whistle or your voice. This takes time, but once you have got it into the dog's mind that it mustn't chase sheep, it will just go through amongst them and never take any notice of them.

If you keep to this simple method of training your dog

and you are consistent with it, by the time it is about fifteen months old, you will be a good deal of the way to having a well-trained obedient working gun dog. Keeping the lessons short and regular is the secret. Remember, your animal is a friend, and should be treated with kindness. Be good to it, but don't give it titbits whilst it is working; its mind will be keyed into its job, and giving it a titbit does nothing for it then. If you wish to give it a treat, wait until lunchtime, then allow it a drink and a little snack. This will also help refresh it for its work in the afternoon.

The co-ordination between trainer and dog is tremendous when working among fur and feather. A good dog will soon find any weakness in the trainer, so remember to be firm with it when you are working in the field. There is no need to use a choke chain for a well-trained dog, for a slip lead is sufficient – I sometimes just loop a piece of cord around my dog's neck when out working. The springer spaniel I have at the moment is a top-notch dog. I started his training when he was just ten weeks old, and I have only missed the odd few days since then. I have even got up during the night and worked a turnip field on the farm with the dog in the moonlight, in order to be consistent with his training. Although this dog has a very strong temperament, he is trained to a very high standard, and it is a pleasure to work with such an intelligent canine friend.

Giving your dog regular training from the start will help to develop its own skills quicker, and will blend with those being taught by the trainer. You will have a top-quality working dog sooner, and the dog will never forget the technique it has learnt.

RUSTY, THE CROSS-BRED TERRIER

I once had a cross-bred terrier dog called Rusty, who was both a super hunter and ratter. We always had rats at Middle Shield Farm when we had dairy cows; they used to live in the cowshed loft above the cattle. At night, they would come down the corner of the wall and run along the water pipe just above the cows, then descend via the pipes into the cows' trough to eat cow cake and get a drink.

Some winter nights after supper, I used to say to Rusty: 'Let's go and get some rats!' So this is what we did. I would go quietly into the cowshed in the dark. Rusty would wait in the passageway, whilst I went in between the cows nearest the hole into the loft. Some of the animals would be lying down. Then my wife, Kathleen, would come into the cowshed and switch on the light, and quickly scarper back into the farmhouse. As soon as the light went on, the rats would climb back up the water pipes and run along the main pipe to where the hole led into the loft. As they ascended the piping, I used to flick them off over the cows' backs with my stick, to where Rusty would be waiting for them. I have seen Rusty with a rat in his mouth and two more rodents coming through the air at him, and, my goodness, he would get them all. I have seen him kill about seven or eight rats in about five minutes. It was great fun.

4

The Temperament of Dogs

Dogs' temperaments are as different as the colours of their coats, and no two are alike in character. Many breeds may all be of the same colour, such as the yellow labrador, but each individual will have some small peculiarities which will identify it from its brothers and sisters.

To train a gun successfully dog to the point where you can take it to any type of shoot or field event without embarrassment, you must start by getting to know the full character of the animal. Only by doing this is it possible to be able to tell the dog what to do in various situations, even if the dog is confronted with something that it has never seen before. The owner or trainer must, to a certain degree, know how the dog will react. It is not always possible to get this right, and I sometimes make mistakes when my dog does something that I thought it wouldn't. For example, I once had a gun dog that would wait until it thought I wasn't paying attention to it, and then sneak off and chase a rabbit that was flushed. It wouldn't pursue it very far, but it took the opportunity when it could to play around while I was concentrating on something else. The dog got severely ticked off for this!

The temperament, peculiarities and alertness are all very important features of a dog, and they should be studied at length if one is to get the best use out of the animal. Anyone considering training a young pup from the start must understand their dog first, or it will end up only half-trained. The owner or trainer may say that the dog is not very good in the field because it chases everything that is flushed and it just runs wild, but it is not all the dog's fault that it has turned out partly useless. The trainer is mainly to blame for not studying it properly and working on its weak points. It may take weeks or months to really master some defects in a dog during its training. In order to get it right, a wise man, who works with his dog all the time, can only benefit from the time he spends working, training and playing with it.

A strong dog with a very highly excitable temperament is not necessarily wild. It may always be raring and pushing to get going, but this is not a fault in the animal. It may be hereditary from one or both of the dog's parents, or this excitable tendency might be traced back within the breed to grandparents or great grandparents. Sometimes the dog may be too closely interbred. But one thing is for sure, training a dog that has a highly strung nature, whatever its breed, will test to the limit a man's patience if he is ultimately to be able to keep the animal under control when it is hunting and working at full stretch. Some people actually enjoy working and training dogs with a determined temperament. The owner or trainer must understand the dog and not, as some people do, thrash it with a stick, or kick it every time it steps out of line. This will only result in failure, a dog that is only half-trained, and probably a frightened animal as well. Most dogs of this nature will need firm handling. Such a dog will also pick up each step of its training quicker than a docile animal, and it will always be eager and willing to move on to the next stage of its training before it has really mastered the first step.

It is very important that you don't let your animal decide how long each step of its training will take. Keep working at each stage until the dog has mastered it, and until it carries out the action automatically while fully under control. You will have heard many times, when out in the shooting field with gun dogs, that so-and-so is absolutely useless with dogs – as soon as he lets his dog off the lead it heads for the next county! You will also have seen a shooter hitting and kicking his dog when it does something wrong. This sort of treatment is totally unacceptable and, anyway, it might well stop the dog from coming back to heel when called, as it won't wish to go back to get kicked! Dogs won't return to their trainer or master if they think they are going to get punished all the time. The owner may be a nice chap, but if he is very severe with his animal, within half an hour of his hitting and kicking it, the dog will probably do something wrong again, and the whole process will be repeated.

I am sure that most shooters with gun dogs will have witnessed dogs being ill-treated when they are out at the various game shoots. One day I was shooting pheasants on the Scottish Borders with some friends, and another guest at the shoot, a well-known person, had a spaniel with him. At the end of each pheasant drive, this chap started kicking his dog. I could stand this no longer, and said to him politely that he was only hurting and injuring the animal. I suggested he gave it a bit more training at home, and this would stop him from getting frustrated

with the dog. This person turned to me and said: 'You are right, Hunter, I must stop kicking him', and he didn't kick it any more that day. I see dogs being ill-treated on various shoots, and the beatings serve no useful purpose at all. In most cases, the dogs are punished for things they don't know they have done wrong. If the owner or trainer had studied their dog's temperament, and worked on the weak points, there would have been no need to punish their dog for something that they should have trained it not to do in the first place. Dogs also respond quicker and better to kindness and firmness from the owner.

This does not mean that a dog shouldn't be punished if it does something wrong. But the only time this should happen is when it knows that it is blameworthy, and that its owner knows this too; for example, if the dog has chased sheep, cattle, rabbits, or run away too far in front. The dog will look to its owner, waiting to see what the next move will be. Both will know the animal must be punished, but the punishment should be in proportion to the crime. If the dog breaks away as you cross a field with sheep or lambs in it, and it begins to chase them, it should be severely punished for this wrong deed. The form of punishment should vary from giving it a good shake, to hitting it with your cap or your hand, or a rolled up newspaper, giving it a good ticking off, raising your voice to the dog, or using a stick on it. It should not escape being punished, or it will take it for granted that it is allowed to behave in this fashion, and will take more liberties in the future.

The best time to punish your animal is as soon as it has

committed its misdeed. It is no good punishing it half an hour afterwards, even if this may be the soonest you can catch it. No matter how cross *you* are, the dog won't know what it's being punished for. I cannot stress enough, punish the dog *only* at the time of its misdemeanour.

The reasons for punishing the dog at the time it has erred, are twofold. One is that the dog has just committed the offence and is being punished at the scene of the crime. It will register immediately that acting like this will only get it into trouble, and after being punished a few times like this will soon learn it is better to conform and behave itself.

It is a good idea to walk to the dog to punish it, for if you call it to heel, the dog will get to know what is in store for it, and may tend not to come back quickly when called to; it may even crawl along the ground on its belly back to heel, because it is afraid. After it has been ticked off, walk away from it several metres before calling it back. You will find the dog will then come bounding back to heel, ashamed of its wrongdoing.

A dog that won't come back to its owner when called to while working in the field needs further training. Punishing it won't remedy this fault; the remedy is to return to the basic training, keeping it within the thirty-metre range. You can use a rope or a piece of cord to help with this problem – the dog probably finds it is more interesting running about, than coming back to heel when called. Take your time with this problem. Use the whistle and your voice, and don't give it titbits to bring it back, otherwise the dog will always be looking for a reward when it comes back to heel.

A dog with a highly excitable temperament is often very intelligent and very strong at the same time. However, it will make mistakes, especially when flushing pheasants over guns. It may run after a rabbit which has just been flushed in front of it, for several metres, and it should be punished for this. It is sometimes wise just to stop it as it turns from chasing the rabbit, call it to heel or walk to it and give it a good ticking off for this misdeed. Reprimanding the dog is sufficient punishment. It may have realized it shouldn't be behaving like this and have turned back itself. It will think twice before it chases one again that day. Remember, dogs are not stupid, they sometimes think way ahead of their owner and are often two steps ahead! Most dogs that do some-thing wrong in the field, know very well what they are doing.

An excitable, intelligent animal will need a lot of working with for the first two years. However, if you are prepared to spend time (and I mean a lot of time) with it, you will end up with a top-class dog, envied by all the sportsmen watching it at work in the field. Keeping on top of the dog and using its energy to your advantage, is very hard, enjoyable work. Gun dogs with a docile tempera-ment can take more handling to train than an excitable dog. With those of a more placid nature, you may have to work very much harder at each step of its education to get the dog to grasp what is required of it. This will require quite a different technique and handling to a livelier animal, or it may end up as a failure.

Dogs, like people, are as different as the days of the

week, and, like people, you just can't lump them all together, and expect them to respond in the same way. If you have trained one successfully, you may need to adapt all you have learned to be equally successful with a different animal. If the dog doesn't respond to a certain lesson it is being taught, study why this is so, and don't be afraid to change your training methods for this particular dog. When you are training gun dogs, remember to be flexible. Some will do things that you have never seen before when you are working with them, and the trainer will always learn something new from each dog! People can reason with one another, and most will respond to kindness and firmness. Dogs and other animals can't reason, but the most stupid or wildest of them will, in time, respond to kindness and firmness. Even a deaf dog can be trained to a certain standard with hand signals.

A few years ago I had an English springer spaniel, which was a very highly strung dog with a very excitable temperament. When I bought him I thought he would turn out to be a bold dog with a mind of his own, but that, handled properly, he would make a top-class working gun dog, and so he did. But he had to be handled properly. The dog was brought up with the family, and he became very protective towards them. However, he had one fault that would have developed if I hadn't stopped it. When anyone strange, or a child, put their hand down to stroke him, he would show his teeth and snatch at them, but he wouldn't take hold and bite them. I knew what the dog was doing, as my wife had caught the dog at it once or twice and used to tell him off and smack him for snapping at people, especially children.

This didn't break the dog's habit. I had never caught him in the act, although I had attempted to do so. My son was eleven years old at the time we had this dog and my daughter fourteen, and they always had friends coming to the house to see them. They were frequently running around between the house and garden, and, as the dog had the free run of both, he had plenty of opportunities to snatch and show his teeth at the children. One afternoon during the summer, when the dog was only a year old, I had him tied up in the garden, and I happened to be working there at the time when a young boy came running outside to visit my son. He was a regular visitor to our house, so the dog knew him. As he passed the dog, I just happened to look round as the lad was walking past and he put his hand forward to stroke the animal. At that moment, the dog moved towards the boy. He was on a two metre cord, and he showed his teeth at the lad and made to snatch at his hand. This is what I had been waiting for! I spoke sharply to the dog and asked him what the hell he was doing, and he knew he had done wrong. I picked up a stick and went over to him and gave him a good thrashing. I then untied him, and shut him up in the conservatory for a few hours. I asked the rest of the family not to go near him, and just let him think about what he had done wrong. The dog was severely punished, and it stopped him from behaving in that way again. I knew the dog's temperament well, and the punishment I meted out to him for this fault was effective in stopping it, and it was given at the correct time. It is very important that working dogs that bite or snap, especially at children, are sorted out, especially if you

Kathleen Adair, the author's wife, with their springer spaniel, Percy. Kathleen was brought up with farm-working collie dogs and gun dogs

A young woman with her golden retrievers. She also keeps Shetland ponies

Game shooters with their dogs on a crisp, frosty morning in Northumberland

A spaniel guarding the pheasants in the boot of an estate car in the farmyard

Two working sheepdogs housed by the roadside on the moors. The dogs are very well looked after and are taken out on the moors to work among the sheep every day

Bill and Pat Colclough. Bill is a gamekeeper on Blanchland Moor in Co. Durham. They live at Penny Pie. Both Bill and Pat work and train their own gun dogs of various breeds

Wenty Beaumont, with his dog, Oscar, at Bywell, near Stocksfield, Northumberland. Wenty is a landowner in south Northumberland

An adder sunning itself out on the moors. They are very common on the moors and can give you a nasty bite

A cock pheasant with a plastic clip on its beak which stops the bird from feather pecking and causes no discomfort. When groups of birds such as pheasants or chickens are kept together they tend to pluck at each other's feathers

The author, Hunter Adair, at home with his springer spaniel called Percy at the end of a pheasant shoot

have a young family and you want to keep the dog. You may have to punish the dog severely for this, and if you are not a strong enough person to sort this problem out, then you will need to get rid of the dog.

I had confidence that I had stopped this dog's bad habit, but my wife wasn't so sure. There was another instance where I gave this animal a severe thrashing, which also stopped the fault. This did not give me any pleasure whatsoever. This was a dog that you couldn't keep disciplining in

this way, or you would have broken his spirit, and spoiled him from working properly and using his own skill when working in the field. The second incident occurred during his morning walk and exercise time. My wife used to take the dog for a walk every morning during the week for about half an hour or so, and I took him out for an hour or so in the evenings. Some of my time with the animal was spent training it. The dog was strong and always eager and ready to go, which was great. My wife used to vary his walks two or three times a week to stop him from getting bored. On one of her walks she passed a small wood where there were normally a few pheasants. I sometimes also went in this direction, occasionally using the wood to train the dog. One evening, my wife said that when she was walking past the wood, the dog dashed in and started hunting on his own initiative. I asked if she called him back with the whistle. She said she had, but that he wouldn't come back until he had worked the wood through to the other end. At the time, the dog was about eighteen months old, and I had been training him to the whistle since he was about ten weeks old. I thought that maybe this incident was a one-off, so I told my wife to let me know if the dog ran off again into the wood without being instructed to do so.

A few evenings later, whilst having tea, my wife said that the dog had run into the wood again that morning, without being told to do so. This dog had got away with it once and thought he would try it on again! If he was left to continue with this habit, he would start going hunting where and when he wanted for his own pleasure. I had spent a great deal of time and effort both training and working with this dog. I wouldn't mind him using his own initiative at the right time when hunting for a wounded or shot bird, but taking himself off into a wood to start hunting for game birds whilst out on his morning walk was not permitted. This had to be stopped, and the sooner the better.

The way I went about sorting out this problem was similar to the way I had tackled his snatching at children:

catch the dog in the act of doing wrong and punish it immediately! I arranged with Kathleen that I would deliberately
go with her and the dog next morning, passing the small
wood. We each had a whistle, and I left my wife in charge
of the dog, whilst I walked a metre or so behind. She
certainly handled the dog well, but as I had done most of
the field training required, I also punished it when required.
The thicket was just off a cart track, with a wire fence
between the track and the wood. As we approached the
area, the dog was about five metres in front of us. As we
passed the end of the wood, the dog continued on the track
for a further few metres, then suddenly dashed off into the
copse. Kathleen blew on her whistle with two sharp pips,
but the dog took no notice of her. At that moment I also
blew on my whistle with two sharp pips, and the dog turned
immediately. Both whistles are the same, but the tones we
both make on them were different and the dog knew this.
As he came to the side of the wood, he looked at me, and
knew he had done wrong. I whistled him to heel, and asked
what he thought he was playing at. I then put him on the
lead, and gave him a good thrashing with my stick. That
was the end of the matter; the dog never ran off again like
that! But, how did the dog know my whistle from my
wife's? My whistling is always stronger, and he knew. He
was playing my wife up for his own enjoyment!

Some gun dogs are very alert all the time, and others
sometimes have to trip over sitting game birds before they
know they are there. Some will even tell you when birds
are lying thirty or forty metres in front (and pointers are
especially good at this). These are dogs with a good nose.

Because an animal has a good nose, it doesn't, however, always mean that it is continually alert. Many gun dogs, when out for a walk with their owners, may just be playing and running around, not really taking much notice of where they are, and what lies ahead. A pheasant or a rabbit may be flushed by the noise of the dog or its handler, and the animal may just lift its head in surprise and have a look, then return to its own amusement of playing around. However, I have had my own dogs out with me playing around and not concentrating, but at the slightest noise or movement around them, they were fully alert. Their instinct and alertness told them that game birds were around, and they should be amongst them. Even when playing, the dog should be lifting its head up from time to time, checking the scent in the air as well as that on the ground.

Some highly intelligent gun dogs, which have been trained and have three or four years' working experience behind them, never seem to think about anything else but food and work. These are good dogs to have! As they are normally so keen on hunting, no matter where you take them their minds are on work all the time. When working on large pheasant shoots, some animals are so keen and alert they want to keep going all the time, and wonder why we have to stop between drives; they just keep looking at me, and you can see them thinking, 'Come on, let's get going!' The ten to fifteen minutes rest between drives, when the guns are put into place for the next drive, enables keen, alert dogs to rest, and they will therefore work much better throughout the day. Don't forget to give your dog a drink at lunch time, to help refresh it for its afternoon work.

Some gun dogs are not all that keen and alert at hunting, and at the end of a pheasant drive will just lie down at their master's feet, and try to drop off to sleep until roused for the next drive. This type of dog may work all right when being pushed along, but at every opportunity it will just want to lie down and not be bothered about hunting or flushing game birds for anybody.

One thing I have learnt over the years is that *all* dogs have some sort of intelligence. It was only when I started to work and train a variety of gun dogs many years ago, that I found out how intelligent each one was. Dogs are, in general, pack animals, and some, if allowed, will try to become the leader, even over humans. Dogs that have this tendency have to be controlled and taught that this is not the case. Some will soon weigh up who is in charge of them, and a very strong dog will test its owner to see how much it can get away with. Once you let it do its own thing, it will keep trying to take advantage of this, and wanting to be the leader. However, dogs thrive on discipline and firmness. They also like a regular routine, with regular mealtimes, preferably once a day in the evening, around teatime. When the dog is around the house, it should know what it can and cannot do. Only then will you have a really happy, mature working dog, for it will feel comfortable and safe if it has its daily routine.

———◆·———

RUSTY IN THE CORN STACKS

A farmer friend of mine used to build stacks of corn when I had Rusty, and on a threshing day he would ask me to come along and bring my dog, as there were plenty of rats around. As the stack was going down, we used to put netting wire around the bottom of it, and Rusty and I would go into the stack bottom. I always wore gloves for this.

My dog and I would have a field day amongst the rats. He would give the rodent one shake, and toss it over his head. He could kill dozens of them in a very short time. I used to catch a rat by the tail, and as it turned to try to bite me, I would pull it up just in front of me, if Rusty hadn't got to it already. When the rodent couldn't bite me, it would start to spin, and kept spinning until I was just left with the skin of its tail. (This is how some rats escape when they are caught by the tail). Rusty would then grab it!

5

The Management of Dogs

The life span of the average working gun dog is seldom what it should be, although the dogs are very rarely neglected – they are far too valuable for that. In many cases, the problem is the opposite. Some gun dogs are slowly killed by kindness, due to overfeeding and lack of sufficient exercise, especially during the summer months when the shooting season is finished. Ignorance of correct management does tend to reduce a dog's working life, and many animals become unfit for work just when experience has made them very useful and efficient at working in the field amongst fur and feather.

Most gun dog owners have their own ideas on suitable accommodation for their animals. The most common fault is that this can be far too small, and if they have an outside run, some dogs hardly have enough room to turn round. Also, the ventilation of many dog kennels has never really been properly thought out, making them either too hot in the summer or too cold in the winter. In some kennels little bedding is provided for the animals, and, even worse, sometimes no water is laid on either! But I have also seen the opposite extreme: water used so freely that the floors are constantly damp, which can lead to rheumatism in its various forms. Dogs don't need water to be left for them all the time, for they will tell you when they want a drink – usually after feeding or playing around. The greatest of care is needed with the dog's diet, exercise and housing. The animal is of so much value to the sportsman, and no servant is more worthy of his keep than a well-trained, obedient gun dog, no matter what his breed or size. The dog should be a good friend to its owner, and the more you work and play with it, the more you will get from your animal.

The co-ordination between master and well-trained gun dog whilst working in the field can give as much pleasure and enjoyment as shooting a few very high pheasants. Whilst some dog-owners are happy just working their dogs at shoots or on grouse moors, others like to shoot as well. However, they all have one thing in common; the pleasure of what they are doing.

Dogs, like humans, can all have their off days, though. A good staple diet for working dogs is a well-balanced meal or biscuits, with all the nutrients, and with the addition of meat, at the ratio of about four parts of the former, to about one part of the latter. Springer spaniels and labradors should be fed around ten to twelve ounces a day, which is quite sufficient for them. There are also some very good, well-balanced dog food mixtures on the market today. I use one, and have found my dogs stay in tip-top condition. With good tinned foods also available, the variety of dog food gives you plenty of choice. The cost of feeding gun dogs should be around £5 to £10 a week. This should be sufficient, as the dog won't thank you if you feed it on steak. A good diet will help keep the dog in good health until old age, and one good meal per day, preferably in the evenings, is sufficient to keep your animal in good health and condition. There is no need to keep food in its dish all the time, as the dog will only get fat and sluggish.

Dogs coming home from the field at the end of a day's work, should return to a lukewarm feed, especially if it is cold weather, and the food should be sufficient to thoroughly appease the dog's appetite. Should your animal return wet and dirty from the field, it should be consigned to a loose box, kennel or a suitable place where straw, sawdust or blanket material is laid on the floor, and where the dog will rub and dry itself. It is not necessary to dry it, if you can provide space and material for the dog to do this itself. For those owners with small houses or flats, or lack of space outside, the dog is often kept in a basket in the corner of the kitchen. In this case, do dry off your animal with some sort of towel or cloth kept especially for them.

Hutch-type kennels (I have even seen them made out of wooden barrels), placed in the open due to lack of space inside, can be quite adequate, and your animal can be perfectly healthy and happy under such conditions if its comfort is studied first. Many dogs kept in such kennels without contiguous runs will have to be tied up most of the time. Never place the dog hutch or kennel away out of sight of what is happening around the house, and do see that it is so situated that the animal can seek sun or shade as required. Be very careful, also, to keep the back of the kennel to the wind, which makes for warmth, and prevents snow and rain from beating in. The structure should also be kept draught-proof, and inspected at regular intervals. If it is to be used in the open during the day, it is worthwhile lining the inside walls with plastic sheeting, to stop any draughts and make the accommodation more comfortable.

Remember that a dog returning from working in the field is often a tired and thirsty one. If the journey is not too long, it is best for the dog to walk home. If, however, it is brought back in a vehicle, it should not be exposed to draughts and cold winds.

It is unwise to coddle a dog, as nothing is gained by it, except a weakening of its stamina. The harder the dog's existence, the better for its health and appetite. Keep the animal's weight down, as it is likely to suffer less illness if lean and fit. It will also work better and longer when out hunting in the field. Nevertheless, a dog should have all the care and attention it needs. On returning from the shooting field or a long walk it should receive everything it needs before its master ever considers food or drink for himself, no matter how wet, dirty or cold both are on their return. (Rule – *dog first*).

FIELD MANAGEMENT

Good management of a dog around the kennel and house rubs off in the field when the gun dog is out working. If you can't control and handle it at home, there is very little chance of doing much with the animal in the field when it is working amongst fur and feather.

Some gun dogs bred to flush and retrieve game, step up a gear when they start working in the field. If the dog is strong-headed, you will need to concentrate and watch it all the time it is hunting and flushing birds when working at large pheasant shoots. Dogs resemble children in many ways: they are quick to gauge the characters of those in charge of them, and swift to take an opportunity to take liberties. Both children and dogs thrive on discipline.

Good gun dogs will always be willing to take risks when out working in the field. As long as the dog knows that you are watching it, and in control, then there is nothing wrong with it showing a bit of its own skills. A young, highly excitable dog at a driven pheasant shoot, seeing its master shoot and drop several birds close at hand, may sometimes lose all self-control, and instantly run in and retrieve one of the dead birds. Having done the wrong thing, the dog knows it will be punished for its misdeed, but it may be determined to have its fun before returning to good behaviour and its punishment. But escape its punishment, it certainly must not! Giving the dog a good ticking off is sufficient for this.

A timid dog may never do anything wrong, but will very seldom be worth its keep. It may be quite good-looking, something of a showpiece, and it is to shows it should probably be relegated. It may be quite good at retrieving fur or feather that is easily seen, but which you could quite easily pick up yourself. However, when it comes to hunting down a wounded bird that has crossed a small stream, and travelled a quarter of a mile away, the dog immediately gives up, and looks to its master for guidance. This is where a dog with a strong temperament, plenty of courage, endurance, discipline, and a first-rate nose will earn its keep; and there is no reason why it can't also be good-looking! It will just need a strong person to control it.

All gun dogs are different to manage, as they have their own little quirks. An owner may purchase a really top-quality working gun dog, the best trained in the country, but if he is an unsuitable handler he will soon spoil it. At the end of the first day of working in the field it may be thoroughly out of control. Certainly within a few weeks it will be so unruly and out of hand as to be unrecognizable as the same dog that was purchased. The owner may have no way with dogs at all, but because he enjoys shooting, considers he would be much better with a gun dog already trained for him, and thinks that the dog should just hunt and retrieve game birds with little management control. This will not happen. Management skills need to be polished all the time.

PLANNING A PHEASANT SHOOT

When you own a pheasant shoot, you have to plan and organize how you are going to shoot and drive the woods. Even on a rough shoot, some organization of the day's sport is necessary, but very often, little thought is given to how the dogs will be managed during the day. Sometimes the day's sport can be utterly spoiled for some participants, because far too little attention is paid to the gun dogs, and, due to the shooters chattering throughout the day, dogs are left running around, thoroughly out of control, and flushing game birds well out of range.

Some owners send their gun dogs to a trainer for several months' schooling during the summer months, and they will return to the owners for the start of the shooting season. The dogs are likely to be in top form, and raring to go. Then, at the end of the season, many dog-owners more or less ignore their gun dogs until the start of the next season, expecting them just to pick up where they left off, and hunt, retrieve and be as steady and obedient as they were when they returned from the trainer. Although gun dogs work only a few months of the year, refresher training is very useful during the close season. Faults will develop if some continuous fundamental field management and training is not persevered with throughout the whole year. The most intelligent of dogs has a very small brain, and can't remember everything it has been taught if it is left for several months without practice. Most sheepdogs are far better trained than many gun dogs, not because they are more intelligent, but because they are working nearly every day of the year, and they get to know what is expected from them as their work is very consistent each day. Some gun dog-owners say they don't have the time that a shepherd has to spend with their dogs. That may be true, but continual discipline and training is very important nonetheless, otherwise the most common faults can arise, and then take weeks to eradicate again. My gun dogs work throughout the whole shooting season. During the summer months I relax their training quite a bit, although I still keep keyed into the minds of the dogs, and we are on the same wavelength. I still put them through training sessions to keep them on their toes. Then, a month or so before the shooting season starts, I give them regular refresher training sessions, just to polish them up before they start working amongst the game birds.

My father was great with dogs – better than I am, although a lot of his training and management skills have rubbed off onto me. I can well remember how in the 1940s he used to hatch and rear about fifty young pheasants a year, and then invite some of the local lairds and lassies along for a bit of shooting. The young pheasants were fed on porridge. (Come to think about it, everything was fed on porridge in the mornings: dogs, cats, ducks, chickens, the young pheasants, and humans – if you were alive and breathing, you got fed porridge with salt! It is great stuff with some cream.) My mother also used to hard boil a few hens' eggs, and chop them up with a bit of butter, salt and pepper, and the young pheasants got a feed of this about three days a week. As they grew, they still got their porridge in the mornings with salt. Then they would be fed on oats and bean meal, which was crushed on the farm (the latter was very high in protein). The birds seemed to do very well, and not many young ones died; probably the porridge they got made them strong and sturdy. On the shoot days, I had the job of carrying the game. When I was about ten years old, carrying three hares over rough ground was quite a haul, but it was great fun. My father would have two or three days' shooting, and there would be about six guns. Looking at the records, the bag for a day was eleven pheasants, five hares, two snipe and a mallard duck. After each shoot, the guests were invited back to our house for something to eat. My mother was a really good straightforward cook, and her food was always delicious: mince, mashed potatoes, and mashed turnip would be the main

course, followed by a clutty (cloutie) pudding – a gorgeous steamed fruit-pudding. There was always plenty to drink. My interest in gun dogs, game shooting and wildlife comes from my father, and what a great tutor he was. He made us all toe the line, and eat our porridge!

One of the faults that most commonly returns during the close season in the summer months is that the dog keeps running too far ahead before turning back. When the new season starts, it will charge ahead, flushing all the game birds and spoiling the shooting for most of the guests that day. It can be very difficult to correct this, and to get the animal back within the thirty-metre range. The longer the dog is allowed to range too far in front, the more difficult it is to correct it; it may even take a whole year to sort out the problem. Remember, gun dogs are bred to hunt, and it is only *where* they hunt that you want to control. The answer is not to let the fault develop in the first place. I seem to keep harping on about this, but I have seen the problem so often. Even well-trained, obedient gun dogs will, from time to time, break the rules and charge away out in front. My father used to tie up one of the dog's front legs at some training sessions, particularly if it was a very strong, bold dog, so that he could, by this method, keep the dog's attention and steady it down. Shepherds also use this method when training a strong-headed collie which runs away out of control whilst it is amongst sheep. I have tried this myself with a strong-headed gun dog, to try to get into its mind to slow it down, but kept the training lessons very short. This is a very strong measure to take, and I wouldn't recommend it. To return to basic training within the thirty-metre range on a regular basis is still the most effective way of eradicating this fault.

——•◆•——

TRAINING TERRIERS TO CATCH RATS

A rat catcher friend of mine in the north used to catch the rats on some cargo ships that arrived in the Tyne Docks, carrying timber or grain. The ships had to be docked for about ten days or so. He caught the rats for half an old penny (about a fifth of a new penny) per rat, drown most of them, and then sell some alive to the miners for one old penny a rat. The miners used them to train their terrier dogs as rat catchers. Some of them asked my friend to pull out the teeth of the live rats first for the same price, so that the rats couldn't bite their dogs!

6

Dogs on a Grouse Moor

One day, a grouse-moor-owner friend of mine and I were both working our gun dogs, looking for a grouse he had shot. He remarked that 'You need a pack of dogs when working a grouse moor in order to cover the ground properly'. There is some truth in what he said – and he said it because it was taking quite a time to find his dead bird. Nonetheless, a good gun dog, or a pair of good dogs, will normally be able to find all the shot birds, though it may take some time to pick them all up. On some moors, the heather is very thick and long, and when a shot grouse drops into cover like this it can take some finding, even for the best of dogs, as the vegetation can be knee deep.

WALKING UP

When shooting grouse over dogs, there are several important points to take into consideration. The direction of the wind should always be studied, and the drives should be arranged accordingly. Most grouse will quickly be off if the dogs try to point them, or flush them downwind. However, when flushing grouse over the dogs, the terrain on some hills and moors may not always be suitable for driving them into the wind.

Some knowledge of grouse and their habits will also help to ensure a fairly good number of birds for the dogs to flush or point and, at the end of the day, the guns will end up with a bigger bag. Grouse are birds of habit, and in the

early morning they will normally be at their feeding ground. This is on heather that is anything from three to four years old, and they may eat there for several hours. Such youngish heather is not very dense, and if you approach the birds in their feeding area with dogs, they will tend to run for cover among the thicker heather nearby. Some will hide and wait for the dogs to either point or flush them, but others will lie and then fly off in a pack, or in ones or twos.

After feeding in the morning, the grouse will then fly off to their roosting ground, which may be several miles away, depending a great deal on the nature of the ground. They will spend most of the middle hours of the day in this area, sometimes sitting around in family packs. Quite a number of birds may be flushed from the roosting area at the same time when you are shooting grouse over dogs. It may be the third drive in the morning when the guns are walking this sector, and strict silence should be the order of the day. It may also pay to keep the dogs to heel if the grouse are really wild, and lift in several packs at a time. The guns should be kept in line, and asked to walk the ground slowly.

In the evening, the grouse will return to their feeding ground and spend the last few hours of the day there before returning to the roosting ground. The dogs may point or flush the same birds two or three times in the day, depending on how long the guns spend on the moor, and the distance they have walked.

Weather also plays a great part in where the grouse can be found on the moors and hills. For instance, on a blustery windy day the grouse may be found on the lee side of hills, seeking shelter. In very wet weather the birds will normally make for the high ground governed by their survival instinct. During the nesting season, sometimes the grouse that nest on the lower ground get caught out by long spells of heavy rain and freak thunderstorms, and the eggs can get washed out. Sometimes, several young chicks get drowned in ruts if the wet weather continues for days and weeks at a time. During very hot weather in the summer, the grouse will often frequent the sides of burns and streams, and will seek cover amongst mixed bracken and heather near to water.

Depending on how many grouse are on the moor, the dog-handler should work his dog accordingly. If, for instance, grouse are few and far between, the dogs can be allowed to range a little further out, but no further than around the thirty-metre range. They should also be made to cover the ground thoroughly, and should not be allowed to tear away in front, out of gun range. The outside beats on the moors and hills should always be worked first, to drive the grouse to the middle and lower parts of the moor for the afternoon shooting.

Working a grouse moor or hills with dogs is very hard work, and the dogs should not be allowed to hunt around when there is nothing to hunt for. Always keep them as fresh as you can, and rest them when possible. When the day is very hot, the dogs should be allowed a drink of fresh water from time to time, and a flask or can should be carried for them. Also, offer them a snack at lunch time if they will eat it. Some dogs won't eat anything when they are out working, although they will have a drink. Some very young, inexperienced, or very old dogs may have to be changed at lunch time, so as not to overwork them. This depends a great deal on the weather, as some very keen animals will work until they drop, if you let them.

If you are working your spaniels or labradors on the moor between two guns, you must have some method of attracting the guns' attention when a bird is flushed. One of the shooters may have a dog of his own, which may be a setter or a pointer, and he can't watch his own dog and others at the same time. Some grouse can be very difficult to see, as they lift and skim the ground in front of the dogs and guns. It is no use calling 'A bird on your left' to the gun on that side when the bird is about a hundred metres or so in front of him. Apart from the time it takes to say the whole sentence, another bird may have lifted, and you will be making too much noise anyway. A simple communication system is needed between the dog, men and the guns, and this should be agreed upon before the shooting starts. For instance, use simple language when a bird lifts, such as 'Mark right', 'Mark left', or 'Mark behind'. The dog men should always be very polite to the guns, as they may be paying a lot of money for the privilege of shooting the grouse, but your concentration should be on your animal, as you may have to steady it if the grouse start lifting in large packs.

I can well remember one fine day I was working a labrador dog on a grouse moor in Scotland. They were shooting the birds over dogs, and my father was one of the guns that day. I was working my dog between a young gentleman who was a regular at the shoots, and a gentleman in his seventies who was a guest. The game-keeper instructed me to work between them with my dog on all the drives. I agreed with both guns that my call would be simply 'Bird left', 'Bird right', or 'Bird forward', as the grouse lifted. The young gentleman had a black labrador, and as I had worked the moors and shot with him before, I knew his methods. I had never seen the older chap before. I am always very cautious when walking with guns on a grouse moor that I don't know, because if a bird is flushed, and breaks back between the stranger and me, his instinct may be to swing his gun through the line and frighten the daylights out of me!

It was not long before my mind was put at rest as we walked the hundred-odd metres to the moor to line up. I was to learn from the young gentleman that this elderly man shot a great deal; in fact, he owned both a grouse moor and a pheasant shoot. I was, however, to learn a great deal more about our shooting friend when we started walking the moor. The older chap was walking on my left, and we hadn't walked very far when my dog flushed two grouse, which broke off to the left. I called 'Birds left'. The old chap had a shot at the second bird, which in my eyes was well out of range before he lifted his gun. The same thing happened to several other birds on the drive, for the grouse lifting at my feet were out of range before he saw them. At the end of the first drive, he had bagged a brace of grouse, when he should have shot at least ten or twelve birds. I politely asked him if he didn't hear me calling. He replied, 'My dear friend, my hearing aid is a bit dickey today.' I had no answer to that.

If the scent is bad on the moor, then work the dogs close at hand, and make sure the ground is worked thoroughly and slowly. Some dogs will want to push ahead to try to find some grouse, but don't let them. Should you happen to be working with labradors or spaniels, and a number of

birds are being shot, pick up the dead ones you can see yourself, and let the dogs hunt for the difficult ones.

PICKING UP BEHIND THE BUTTS

To be out on a grouse moor on a warm, still day during the months of August and September is delightful, for the wild, open spaces and the stillness have a great charm which is difficult to find anywhere else. Seeing and hearing this unique dark bird flying fast just above the skyline, and over one's head, sometimes in packs, is enchanting.

The heather is very hard on the dogs' feet, and if you are working the moors quite a lot early in the season, I would advise you to give your gun dogs some road work before the 'glorious twelfth' in order to harden their pads.

Picking up shot grouse behind the butts and marking where the birds fall is thrilling work for a dog-handler. If there are a lot of grouse being shot that drop behind the butts, it is better to mark on a card with pencil or pen where the birds fall. Put a cross where each shot grouse dropped, then at the end of the drive have a look at your card and decide how you are going to pick up the dead birds with your dog. I prefer to work my dog to the nearest dead bird first, which is normally the bird furthest away from the butts. Remember to use the wind direction, as this will help the dog to find the dead grouse more quickly; I always check this first, so that I can work my dog up wind, which gives it a much better chance for a quick retrieve. I then work my way towards the butts to see if there are any other shot birds which haven't been picked up. By the time I have arrived at the butts, the beaters will probably have moved on to start the next drive, but sometimes there are still one or two dead birds around, which take a lot of finding.

There is something special about standing or sitting away out on a grouse moor behind the butts, watching the shooters and the grouse, as one waits with one's dog for the beaters to start driving the grouse towards the butts. There is a creepy, eerie feeling about the wildness of the open moors, which you don't experience anywhere else. The stillness is just so peaceful and quiet.

Some grouse can travel a long distance behind the butts after they have been shot, and if the bird is only wounded it can travel up to a mile or so from the butts before dropping to the ground. It may then run for a long distance, before it finally takes cover amongst some thick heather. A wounded bird some distance out can take some finding with a dog. The dog-handler will hunt and hunt, until the animal finds it.

The main reason for acquiring the skill of picking up shot grouse behind the butts with gun dogs, is to assist the shooters in marking the birds they have shot, and help them pick up the birds that fall behind the butts. The wielder of the gun may not see all the birds falling, if he or she is kept busy shooting. If the grouse come over the butts in pairs or singles, then the shooters will normally manage to mark the birds they hit themselves. However, when the grouse come over in packs they are firing at birds both in front of them and behind the butts. They then have more difficulty in marking where all their birds have dropped. This is where the dog-handler comes in, for he or she may be standing or sitting some 150 metres or so behind the butts, and should then have a panoramic view of what is going on in the butts and the surrounding area.

The gun dogs behind the butts on a grouse moor play a different sort of role to those picking up pheasants behind the guns. The pheasants will lift and climb up into the sky, and the dog-handler will usually be closer to the guns than when on a moor. Because of this, he will be in a much better position to mark the pheasants that drop, although wounded birds can sometimes run a long way before they stop.

I don't think it is very wise to let the dog have too many retrieves, which may bore it, especially if it is still young. I sometimes get the dog to find the shot birds for me when there are a lot of dead grouse to retrieve, and then pick them up myself. Should there still be more shot birds to find and pick up at the end of a drive, other dog-handlers may be called to come and help recover all the birds quickly, as the same butts may be used for the next return drive.

On some grouse moors in the north, a row of grouse butts may be used for two drives, depending on the lie of the land, and at the end of the first drive the dog men have to retrieve the shot birds as swiftly as possible.

Grouse are very shy birds, but they tend to fly low, and they have such an erratic movement in flight, with their amazing ups and downs, that the dog-handler should be stationed well out of gun range during the drive, as the bird may dive and swerve between the butts and the guns, so that the latter may be shooting at birds just the height of a man! The thrill and difficulty of shooting driven grouse has made them something of a unique bird, which they are likely to remain. The pleasure lies in the sport, the surroundings, and working one's dog or dogs amongst them.

Because of the distances involved, with the dog and handler well behind the butts, sometimes the animal does not see the grouse coming over. Even the butts may be out of sight, as the handler may be standing amongst old, thick, rank heather, and therefore the lie of the land may put the butts out of the dog's view. The dog will see the birds flying over its head, and may also mark a grouse if it drops nearby, but in general, most of the birds that are shot and drop well behind will have to be hunted for. The grouse that drop near the butts will probably be picked up by the guns there, some of whom will have their own dogs, and they may then come and help the dog men to look for the shot birds behind them.

One thing I have learnt about working gun dogs at game shoots: never to take it for granted that, because the landowner has invited me along to a shoot to work my gun dogs, I have the right to pick up any of his guests' shot birds. I would soon be in trouble! Some shooters get as much pleasure and enjoyment out of seeing their gun dogs retrieving the game, as they do from actually shooting the birds. So, remember that permission is needed before retrieving other people's game.

I can well remember one day I was at a grouse shoot with my father. He was shooting, and I was in the butts with him, but he was picking up the birds he shot. I had a young labrador at the time which I was training, and I was eager to get the dog amongst the birds. This was the third drive of the morning. My father and I were both in the second butt from the left-hand side. In the end butt was a fairly elderly lady, also shooting, who had her springer spaniel with her. I had never seen her before, but I was soon to know who she was. At the end of the drive, only one bird was shot, and this lady had been the successful one; the dead bird had dropped behind the two butts, and was lying right in the middle between them. When the beaters came in and the drive was finished, I thought I would work my dog out to find and retrieve this single grouse, thinking I would also be doing

a good job for the lady as well. My dog had just picked up the bird, and was fetching it back to me, when I heard the lady's voice behind me, asking me what I thought I was doing by picking up her bird. She said I should mind my own business, and leave her bird alone. I said I was sorry, and thought she wouldn't mind me picking it up for her, but she said in future that I was not to touch any of her birds unless she asked me for assistance. A lesson I was never to forget! My father knew this lady well, and told me it was normally her husband that came grouse shooting, but that he had been ill, and she had turned up in his place that day. My father also politely told me off for what I had done, but also said that making mistakes was sometimes the best way to learn. I was so eager to get my young dog working that I had missed the fact that the lady also had a young dog with her, and she was eager, too, to get a retrieve for it. As the day wore on, this lady tried very hard to be friends with me. At the end of the day, she thanked me very much for helping her, and hoped to see me again soon. Although, since this time, other people's gun dogs have picked up my shot game without being asked to, I never say anything to them as long as my own dog gets a retrieve or two. It is normally dogs which are badly trained that act like this, and dash in and pick up anybody's shot game birds.

———•◆•———

I can remember that we had a nasty-natured, sly collie dog tied up in the cow byre. My mother used to feed it once a day with porridge. This sly animal sometimes used to get a mouthful of it, then scatter it around within its chain length. Then, whenever a chicken came into the byre to eat the porridge, the dog would have it when it came within range. A few days later, the dog would get porridge, and some chicken bones!

Standing guns at a pheasant shoot waiting for the pheasants being flushed over them

The game shooters returning from a pheasant drive at lunchtime near the Scottish border

The woodcock is a mysterious little bird and has been hunted for centuries by man. The tip feathers on the woodcock's wings are very hard and sharp and are used by artists

The author on his farm at
Hexham in Northumberland

Dog with a mallard duck.
The author often uses a
mallard duck for dog
training sessions

This particular dog was an excellent gun dog and extremely intelligent

Two gamekeepers on a shoot in the north

The kestrel is a lovely bird of prey which is also known as the windhover due to its habit of hanging motionless in the air, with its head to the wind about 4 or 5 metres above the ground hunting for mice and voles

A pair of working dogs – a golden retriever and an English springer spaniel

Farm dogs in the back of a pick-up. Many farm dogs are used to sitting in open farm pick-ups or on tractors, trailers or quad bikes while moving around the farm

7

Dogs on a Pheasant Shoot

Pheasants are the most widespread game birds in the world. They were first introduced into this country from Asia, around nine hundred years ago. The most common pheasant is the Old English type, the male bird sporting a metallic green head and neck. However, other varieties of pheasant were also introduced later from the Far East, such as the green pheasant, or the pheasants with the white neck ring and lower back. Many pheasants have also been interbred, not only with the Old English type, but with other subspecies which were introduced from time to time. This has resulted in a wide variety of various coloured birds both in Britain, as well as much of western Europe.

There are many game farms now in existence in this country, but very few country estates still hatch their own pheasants. Instead, they buy in young birds, from week-old chicks, to six- or eight-week-old poults. Most week-old pheasant chicks still need warmth, and many gamekeepers now use gas cylinders for heating the chick houses.

Pheasant-rearing is a great deal easier in many ways than it looks. Some forty-odd years ago many great shoots and estates hatched and reared their own birds with the help of broody hens, or clockers as they were known, either bought or loaned from the farmers in the neighbourhood. Nevertheless, pheasant rearing is time-consuming while the birds are very young, because they take a great deal of daily attention. As the birds grow older, and are penned in the woods, they also require protection from predators such as foxes.

When the pheasants are finally released into the woods from the pens, they still take a great deal of management, with daily feeding, and strenuous efforts to keep them from straying. The size of the shoot and the types of woods and coverts provided for the pheasants will affect how well you can hold them on the shoot; they can be beggars for straying if the conditions are not right for them. They don't like dark woods or coverts, but prefer open, warm ones, with some dry ground cover. Fir or spruce trees, with the branches lopped off at the bottom of them, make ideal good dry ground cover. Lopping the trees also makes the woods easier for the beaters to walk through when they are flushing the pheasants forward to the guns. Brambles also make good ground cover, as well as rhododendrons. Pheasants nearly always make for the sunny side of the woods and coverts, and therefore, when they stray, they will invariably head south or west. However, they can be encouraged not to stray off if plenty of food is around, and there is little disturbance by vermin.

FLUSHING PHEASANTS FROM COVERTS

Beating and flushing pheasants from coverts over the guns is very hard work. All the more so if you have a young, excitable dog to handle, and this is the first shoot of the season on ground where several hundred pheasants have been reared. Normally, most gun dogs, no matter how well they have been trained, will not see and be confronted with as many game birds at one time as at the first large pheasant shoot. Proper control is very important,

as mistakes are almost bound to happen, even with the best trained dogs. The temptation for the dogs to run riot amongst the birds is considerable, and they can take some holding back.

There are several principles involved in beating and flushing pheasants towards standing guns. One is to get the birds to lift and fly high and fast over the guns, but not too many at a time, in order to give the guns time to fire and then reload. When working a covert along with the beaters, I like to work my dog no more than 20 metres or so inside it from the hedge side or wood edge for several reasons. I always find the beaters without dogs are inclined to walk through the thicket much faster than the dog-handlers, and with all the shouting that goes on, the dog may not always pick up its instructions. With a young gun dog, it is very important that it can hear its handler all the time, especially if there are a lot of pheasants about, and it is very noisy.

I don't particularly like working my dog along the inside of a covert, mainly because the animal is inclined to run along the wood edge, where there is often fairly thick ground cover. Many hand-reared pheasants will either run to the end of the covert before they lift, or else make for the edge and hide. I train my dogs to quarter the ground, and sometimes they will tend to keep going forward along a wood edge, flushing the birds, and before I know it, the dog is away in front, well outside the thirty-metre training range. It is very important not to let it work a boundary away forward. It must still quarter its ground and, in fact, on shoots where several hundred pheasants have been released, the handler should take it steady, and work the covert thoroughly. The dog should be made to work tight to his handler, quartering every foot of the ground, especially where the undergrowth is very thick. Quartering may be difficult if there are many pheasants about, for the dog will be flushing birds every few yards on either side of the handler, right through to the end of the covert.

The animal may sometimes get on the down-drive side of a shrub or a few branches which are lying tight to the ground, so that the birds are flushed back to the handler, instead of going forward. But this may be the only way the dog can get into thick cover, and, if it has any intelligence, it should look for the easiest way to get in. Sometimes the birds may press further into concealment, becoming trapped in the process. This may result in the dog being unable to flush the birds, especially if there is only one small access into this area, and the dog is blocking it. The dog should then be called off immediately and the birds released by hand.

When pheasants are flushed back from tight cover, the dog-handler should try and turn the birds towards the guns. Pheasants turned back in this fashion will be climbing, and should provide some high, sporting shots for the guns. As the beaters progress through the covert, many reared pheasants will run forward and, if the gamekeeper has a flushing point, there may be some wire netting right across it, some thirty metres or so from the end of the copse. Some birds will stop as they reach the wire and then run backwards and forwards along the bottom of it. Some will lift, but the bulk will just wait. As the beaters and dog men approach the flushing wire, the dogs must not be allowed to run in on the birds and flush them all at once. They should be put on leads instead.

A gun dog that sees pheasants running forward will be eager to chase after them, so it is better to stop it, and let the gamekeeper walk forward, attempting to flush a few birds forward at a time. When most have been driven out at the wire, some will have hopped over, and run on. The dogs can then work the ground, as some of the birds will just sit tight and not move unless lifted by the dogs following up their scent. Some will even sit so tight to the ground that the beaters can walk past within a few inches and the birds will not lift! It takes a good gun dog to shift them!

On the far side of the flushing wire, the cover should always be fairly open, to let the birds fly up and out. Many coverts are far too thick, so the pheasants find it difficult to do this. Some will then just run forward, or out at the sides. Over the wire, the beaters will get lined up ready to beat out the final thirty odd metres or so to the end of the copse. The gamekeeper may have a pheasant feeder just a few metres from the end, and there will be many birds around that area, including those who have hopped over the wire. The beaters and dog men then have to work out the best way to advance. If there is little ground cover, it may be better to keep the dog at heel, or on a lead if it is prone to get carried away by the excitement. Or the gamekeeper or beater in charge may ask the handlers to let off their dogs and hunt out the rest of the covert. You have to know your dog and its abilities, though, for you will not be popular if your animal runs riot amongst the birds at this point, sending them all scattering out at the end at the same time. The shoot-owner may well make it known that he is not pleased!

A good gamekeeper will know the beaters and the dog-handlers, and which ones can control their dogs adequately. It is very good experience for a young dog to be on a lead, and just stand and watch all the commotion when there are a lot of pheasants at the end of the covert. At the end of each drive, the dog-handlers should look at the standing guns to see if there is one that hasn't a dog with him or her. They may then get the chance to pick up one or two shot birds. Remember, if you have a young gun dog for which you want to get one or two retrieves, always be wise, and have a polite word with one or two guns to ask their permission first. Should one agree, it would be a good idea to get yourself into a position during the next few drives by beating and working your animal nearest where the gun is standing shooting, so that you have the chance of picking up his shot birds with your dog. A word in the gamekeeper's ear is also advisable. A walking gun moving outside the covert but in line with the beaters may shoot a pheasant that is going back, and which drops behind the beating line. The gamekeeper may then ask you to turn back, to try and pick it up with your dog. Try to mark where you see the bird fall. Then, don't just walk straight to where it dropped, but make your dog work the ground back, so that it finds it for itself. You will notice at most large game shoots that there is normally a handler picking up dead or wounded birds in coverts, after the beaters and guns have moved on to the next drive. If you are a good team with your animal, you may be asked to become a regular beater at some shoots, picking up the runners and wounded birds after the drives. You can then take plenty of time working your dog to the best of its ability, and get a lot of pleasure from it.

FLUSHING PHEASANTS FROM ROOT CROPS

Pheasants feeding in stubble fields, or on open ground, always like to be near cover, and if they are disturbed they will soon be out of sight, making for home and cover. Where root crops, such as turnips, kale, potatoes, or a game crop are grown beside a wood where pheasants have been released, the birds will be in amongst the crops in large numbers, especially on fine, sunny, dry days. They don't particularly like wet root crops, so, on an inclement day, you will find them gathering at the edges of the woods. Even so, whatever the weather, you will always find some birds amongst the root crops.

On a fairly dry day, pheasants like nothing better then scratching amongst root crops, as they have cover to hide in, and they also like picking amongst the various seeds and other weeds and grasses. When flushing them from root crops with dogs, the same principles apply as in flushing them from woods and coverts. Try to get the birds to lift and fly high and fast over the guns. Great care should always be taken that dogs don't tear away through the root crops, flushing all the birds before the guns and beaters have moved into place. Dogs working in roots will usually be able to see the birds being shot, and dropping. Some will be very tempted to push forward towards the action and forget about quartering the crop. This situation can test the steadiest and most obedient of dogs. Pull your animal up straight away, and call it back to heel until the excitement has died down (if there are quite a number of birds lifting at the same time, the guns will have plenty to

shoot at, and be having some fun). You can then start the dog off quartering the ground again. This practice of stopping the animal from time to time, and calling it back to heel when it is working at full stretch, instils discipline, and helps to steady it.

Where a root crop is grown near a wood in which pheasants have been reared, and the crop lies higher, the birds can be flushed in the direction away from the wood, rather than towards it. They will fly back home over the beaters' heads, and if the guns are out lined behind, they will get some very high sporting birds. Driving pheasants away from the guns and from home successfully requires several stops along the edges of the root crop, and at the far end, to try to turn back any birds that want to fly forward, and foil those that try to break out at the sides. When the pheasants are being flushed back over the dog's head, it should quarter the ground as if flushing them forward, and care should be taken that it doesn't break back behind the beating line to retrieve a shot bird. The beaters should walk slowly through the crop, stopping and looking back from time to time to see the birds flying back over, and hoping to see a really high pheasant or two being shot. The dog will also look back as the birds fly over, and it may mark a shot bird falling. If the beaters have just started drawing the root crop, one or two shot birds may fall between the guns and beaters; this is where the dog, if not properly controlled, may break back to pick up one of the shot pheasants.

FAULTS WITH DOGS ON LARGE SHOOTS

Taking a young gun dog to several pheasant shoots can cause the dog to develop various faults if the handler doesn't check them.

During a drive in a wood where there is a large number of birds, one or two may get trapped under some small branches, or in a wire fence, so that the dog is not able to flush them. It may then dash in and grab and kill the birds. This is a bad fault, if left to develop, as the dog may think that it is supposed to catch and kill birds, rather than flushing them. Action should be taken immediately to stop this, although it may be very difficult to get on top of the dog just when it is about to offend. It is better to keep working the dog close at hand, if possible, on a large shoot where hundreds of pheasants have been reared. When birds are trapped on the ground, call the dog off straight away. If it is fully concentrating, and is halfway under some branches, it may not hear, and so may not take any notice of its handler. Step in and stop the dog at once if you can, punishing it for not coming when called. If the dog continues this practice, it will make it hard-mouthed, and it will crush the game birds it retrieves.

Another fault may occur when you are working your gun dog on a drive where pheasants are sitting tight every few metres. The dog can get so excited that it may run past sitting birds, not flushing them and working the ground as it was trained to do. It will be inclined to want to push forward as the birds are being flushed, and, if not watched, will be well away out in front, missing half the pheasants as it charges forward.

When you are training a gun dog to quarter the ground, it may take a long time for it to work the ground automatically. Always try to vary its training ground. You can use the beach, a park, a wood, or an area of rough ground for training – though always use open ground, or woods and coverts where you can see the dog working all the time. On some training sessions, it may flush a hare or a few pheasants from time to time. This is good for it, as the trainer can steady it, and get it to work fully to command as the dog gains experience.

It is very easy to spoil a young gun dog on a large shoot by being tempted to give it more scope than in training sessions. The dog should, in fact, be worked tighter to his trainer in these conditions where pheasants are reared, as the birds will be sitting closer together than

on a rough shoot, where there are only a few game birds about. You may be invited to various game shoots if you are known to be the owner of a good working gun dog, for a good animal is better than three beaters. But don't get carried away at any of these shoots, or give your dog more liberties, because you are amongst strangers; it will take more handling where birds are plentiful, so keep on top of it all the time.

I have worked and studied many gun dogs at large and at small game shoots, as well as on many rough shoots. All have to learn their craft at working amongst game birds. The more work a dog does with them, the better and quicker it will learn its trade. Some, however, will be better than others, no matter how much training and work they get.

When most gun dogs are about six years old, and have been working most shooting seasons, they should have served their time and learned their craft. How good a dog is will depend a great deal on its trainer. I often liken gundogs to professional people: as most adults will know, some professionals are much better at their jobs than others, even if they have served the same length of time at their work. Most gun dogs have faults of one sort or another, but if you have a fairly good dog, it is worth putting up with its faults, as long as they are not too bad. However, if a dog can't be trusted, and keeps biting people, especially children, then, no matter how good it is at field work, get rid of it quickly.

WALKING UP PHEASANTS

When I am walking up pheasants on a rough shoot, and my dog has to work to find and flush the game birds, and then retrieve them when shot, this is completely different from finding and retrieving dead birds at a driven pheasant shoot. On a rough shoot I never know if the dog will find any fur or feather to flush.

It is always wise to keep working your dog close to you when shooting birds over the dog's head, and it is even more important for your animal to be working close at hand if it flushes a hare or a rabbit. If your dog is working away out some forty metres or so in front when a hare is flushed, there is a great risk of your animal being shot, and good gun dogs are too valuable to put at risk. There is an old saying which, 'if in doubt, don't shoot'. However, a number of gun dogs still get shot every season when chasing hares and rabbits, as they are inclined to pursue them, often keeping close on the heels of their prey.

Most dogs are only hit with a pellet or two, but it is still very dangerous to let them hunt out too far in front on a rough shoot. The shooter may think that if he doesn't have a shot quickly, the game will be out of range, and it can all happen so suddenly, as most gun accidents do. I never shoot at a hare or rabbit if a dog is chasing it; there is always the risk of shooting the dog, for the quarry often changes direction suddenly as an evasion technique. And a hare will frequently double back amongst the shooters, which also puts them at risk if someone lifts his gun to try to shoot the hare!

A friend of mine had a lurcher dog that was good at catching hares. The latter are very clever animals for weaving and turning when being hunted. Many times, I have seen hare just at the point of being caught by the animal, and it would suddenly turn and leave the dog standing. A field in front of our house was fairly flat for about one hundred metres or so, then it sloped away down into a dene. The slope was very steep, and couldn't be ploughed, so was just grazed with cattle. It was south-facing, and there were rushes and also long grass in the dene, which was good cover for hares. An old jack hare used to live amongst these rushes. We had

had him for many years, and when my friend came to visit us about once every two or three months, he brought his lurcher dog with him, and we always went down to the dene where he worked the animal amongst the rushes to flush the hare, and see if the dog could catch him.

The old jack hare was far too clever to be caught by any stupid lurcher dog. When the dog flushed it, the hare made up the hill to the flat ground, with the lurcher chasing after it. The hare used to stay on the flat ground for several minutes, swerving and turning with the dog in close pursuit. The hare was in full control of the chase! When it got fed up with being pursued, it used to run straight down the steep part of the dene almost to the foot of it, which was about one hundred and fifty metres down, with the lurcher hot on its tail. When it had almost

reached the bottom of the dene, it would turn quickly, and head straight back up the steep hill, leaving the lurcher stranded. With the hare having such quick acceleration, it was up and over the top and away, before the lurcher had turned round at the base of the dene. My friend and I watched this jack hare escape the dog several times by this method, and the lurcher never had the sense to see that the hare had the chase weighed up and under control.

Many times, when I am walking a rough shoot and shooting pheasants at the same time, it can be very difficult, especially if the ground cover is thick and fairly tall. The dog may flush a pheasant from this area which takes off at forty-five degrees, and as the bird weaves through the undergrowth to get out, it can be a difficult shot if I can't get a clear view of it.

There are many disused railway tracks which have been left to grow back to the wild, and many of these are suitable places for wildlife and game birds. If you happen to have part of an old track on your shoot, they are ideal places for pheasants if you feed the birds, because many parts of the track are very dry and sheltered. A feeder placed every eighty metres or so will attract wild pheasants and partridges and, if the track is fenced off from cattle and sheep, it will improve the ground cover, and allow it to thicken, which in turn will provide much better refuge for wildlife and game.

An old railway track with an embankment on either side is ideal for working and training a dog. As the dog hunts the ground along one side of the track, any pheasants flushed will either lift and fly forward along the track or fly across the track, enabling the shooter to have a shot at the bird. The other side of the railway embankment can then be worked on the way back, or, if two dogs are used, both embankments can be worked at the same time.

8

Finding and Retrieving Game

There is nothing more pleasing for any gun dog owner, than to watch his dog finding and retrieving a cock pheasant. The bright plumage of the bird in the dog's mouth is delightful to see as the dog returns to his master with his retrieve over the snow-covered ground.

Most game birds are shot by being driven over the guns, and many gun dogs mark some birds that fall. However, on a blustery day when high birds are flying with the wind, a pheasant that is shot in front and above a gun can carry 50–100 metres behind before it lands on the ground. An experienced gun dog sitting beside his master may mark a bird falling away behind him, but it is unwise for the shooter to send his dog to retrieve the bird. The dog may not find it where it was seen to fall, and if it is left to hunt for the bird, it may take a long time, which will then hold up the rest of the shooting party. It is much better to let the dog-handler, who is picking up behind the guns, deal with birds falling a long way out from the guns. The handler will have plenty of time to spend hunting for the bird with his dog, which may already have marked where the bird fell.

Finding and retrieving shot birds can sometimes test the most experienced dog-handler and the best of gun dogs. When a shoot-owner comes over to the handler at the end of a pheasant drive and says that his friend has shot a bird which he is pretty sure dropped just inside a small scrub wood some fifty metres away, and points in that direction, this sounds like a fairly easy retrieve. However, it is not always so simple, as I have often discovered. First of all, the shoot-owner has more or less convinced the handler that the bird has actually dropped because it was shot, whereas it may just have been gliding, untouched, to the small scrub wood.

This situation actually happened with me this shooting season. The beaters had just drawn through a coppice on the previous drive. The shoot-owner asked me to go back to look for a bird that one of his guests was convinced he had shot, so I dropped down wind into this scrub wood which was only about sixty metres wide and about two hundred metres long. It was quite thick in places, although fairly open at ground level, and I thought my dog wouldn't have much trouble finding the bird. I started working him into the wind, towards where I was told the bird had dropped. I kept working him close to hand to make sure he covered all the ground, and, because the area wasn't very wide, I intended working the dog up one half of the wood, and then back down the other half if need be. I did this four times, and there were no signs of any dead birds! I then started looking up among the trees and shrubs, and there was the bird, stuck in the fork of a small tree some five metres from the ground! I climbed up for it, whilst my dog watched. On this occasion the shoot-owner was right.

When I and my dog are picking up on a large pheasant shoot, I may not know any of the people who are shooting. I may get instructed by one of the guests to go and hunt for a bird he thought he had hit, and he attempts to tell me where he thinks the bird has dropped. I always have to be a good listener, as the shooter will usually think that the bird is dead, and that it has dropped here or there. Although I may not always agree with what I am being told, it is wise to listen and always be polite with the shoot-owner's guests.

If picking up shot birds behind the guns, I try and position myself in a vantage point that enables me to spot the birds that are hit but keep flying on – some of these can glide for several hundred metres before they drop. I am a regular at some pheasant shoots, and know where to position myself in order to see what is happening all around me, and also to keep well out of gun range. At the same time, I take great care that I don't go too close to the ground that will form the next drive and disturb the pheasants there. If it is a shoot at which I am not a frequent visitor, I stay closer to the guns, and keep down when the shooting starts, and I never seem to go far wrong by doing this.

When pheasants are coming fast and high, they normally start losing height once they have passed over the guns, even if they have not been shot. Some will start gliding after they are over the shooters, and some pheasants may skim the ground for quite a long way before landing, whilst other birds change course and glide into the nearest wood or hedgerow. Many guns at driven pheasant shoots are misled by birds gliding for cover after they have passed over the line, with the result that the people with gun dogs are often sent to hunt for a bird that is thought to have been downed, but wasn't. I have often hunted woods and coverts due to this, with little result! Even so, it is always better to work the dog and hunt for a bird that someone thinks is hit, for it will please the shoot-owner, although the dog may get bored if it has nothing to retrieve.

There is always something to learn when working a gun dog at a pheasant shoot. I can well remember one instance: it was the first drive after lunch, and I was well placed up

beside the guns, and could see most of the birds that were being shot. The guns were lined out between two woods on a slight incline. One of the guns quite close to me shot a woodcock which was flying straight over his head. The bird was flying fast as it broke cover from the wood where the beaters were driving through, and it dropped some thirty metres or so behind the guns in the next wood. I was pretty sure it was dead, from the way it was shot and the manner in which it dropped into the wood, and my first thought was that it shouldn't be all that difficult to pick up.

That wood was going to be the next drive, and before the beaters moved into position, the owner of the shoot said to me that they should pick the woodcock as they beat the wood through. I dropped back into the coppice that the beaters had just left, in order to hunt for a cock pheasant that had been shot and dropped in there. The beaters hadn't seen it as they passed through the wood, but my dog soon found it, lying amongst some thick brambles; he more or less told me where the bird was.

At the end of the second drive, the shooters and beaters were discussing how it had gone. When the shoot-owner asked the gamekeeper if they had retrieved the woodcock as they beat the wood through, the latter said that they hadn't seen it, and was the owner sure it was down? The shoot-owner replied that one of his guests had told him he was pretty sure the woodcock was dead. He then came across to me as I was chatting to one of his guests. He asked if I would go and try to find it with my dog. I confirmed that I thought it dead. This is just what a gun dog handler wants: the challenge of hunting and finding a lost game bird. I knew roughly the area where I saw the bird drop, so felt pretty confident. The colour of the woodcock's plumage blends in with the winter surroundings, so it would be easy for the beaters to walk past a dead bird, which would be camouflaged in this terrain. This was a fairly long strip, and it would be about one hundred metres wide. The ground cover was fairly open, although the wood contained a number of small shrubs, and there were a few large fallen trees lying around, which had been there for many years, perhaps damaged or blown over during a storm. I knew the area pretty well, as I had worked it many times before with my dog, and the wood was ideal for working a gun dog – I could see the animal all the time as it quartered the wood like a hoodie crow quartering a grouse moor. I had a springer spaniel at the time which had a few years experience behind him, and if any dog could find the dead woodcock, this dog would if the bird was on the ground or near it.

I decided to work the dog back through the wood in the opposite direction from the beaters. This was against the wind, and would give the dog a better chance of picking up the bird's scent. The beaters and gamekeeper had had four dogs working the wood when they beat it through, which made me think that the bird would be difficult to find. I positioned myself at the end of the wood on the line of where I had seen the woodcock drop, although I was some 150 metres or so from the spot. I worked the dog close, and allowing it to cover about twenty five metres on either side of me. It was a bright afternoon with a slight breeze, which were good conditions for finding a dead woodcock as we worked through the wood. The dog flushed a hen pheasant from the undergrowth, which the beaters had missed.

When we came to the spot where I was sure the woodcock had dropped, the dog was hunting at full stretch, and the ground cover was fairly open, apart from two old rotten trees which were lying on the ground. I stopped where I saw the bird drop, and let the dog hunt around. It was keen enough, but after a few minutes hunting that area, I worked the dog on to the end, but still couldn't find the lost bird. This is where one's knowledge and experience comes in. I had seen the woodcock drop myself, and was sure it was dead (if I hadn't seen the bird being shot and drop, and the shoot-owner or gamekeeper had asked me to hunt for the bird, I would probably have given up when I reached the end of the wood). However, the more I thought about it, the more I was convinced that it was still lying there. My dog had been quite keen at the spot where I thought the bird had fallen, so I decided to work him back to that spot. On arriving there, I thought I would work the dog across that part of the wood, in case the bird was only wounded, and had hopped and fluttered across the coppice. The dog was hunting amongst the two fallen rotten trees, and I kept pushing him on to find the bird, when suddenly he climbed on top of one of the trunks. A branch forked off the fallen tree, and there was a hole at this point. My dog suddenly stopped at this hole, his tail and body wagging furiously. When I looked, there was the missing bird, lying in the hole where it had dropped. Many dogs would never have found it, but I knew my dog would, from all the training and time I had spent working with him.

Recently I was a guest at a driven pheasant shoot, and it is very good discipline for a dog to be trained to sit beside his master, untethered and without moving, whilst pheasants are being flushed over their heads, and some shot around them. A gun dog has to be trained for many jobs, and it will take many years for the dog to be efficient at them all. At this shoot, my dog made a few good retrieves during the morning drives, which I was very pleased about. The pheasants I had shot were all fairly easy for it to pick, and we were both having a good day. During the afternoon, the beaters were driving down one side of a dene, and the shooters were standing in a sort of line at the bottom. The end gun was right beside the river, which flowed down through the dene.

It was a nice quiet afternoon, and I could see the gun standing opposite me up the dene, but I couldn't see the man at the bottom by the river, because the view was blocked by a few small trees. It was so quiet that I could even hear the ripple of the river flowing past! I positioned myself on the slope where I could see any pheasants that came flying down, and my dog sat beside me looking around him.

I hadn't been standing long when the beaters started calling 'Forward', as two pheasants came flying down on my right over the gun above me. He had two shots at the birds, and hit one which fell behind him. A few moments later, a hen pheasant came flying down the dene, making straight for me. As I swung my gun onto the bird, it veered off to my left, making across the river. Just as it was turning, I pulled the trigger. The bird was moving so fast that it carried on across the river, and dropped dead up the other side of the dene. The gun standing down beside the river at the bottom, marked where it had fallen.

The beaters started calling again – by this time they were very close to us, as it was near the end of the drive – and a cock pheasant came flying high and fast down between me and the bottom gun. It was too far out for me to shoot at, and it also started to veer across the river, as we were advised they would do. I heard a shot from the bottom gun, but couldn't see if the bird had dropped, and by this time the beaters were nearing the end of the drive. I made my way down to the riverside, where the bottom gun was standing, hoping to get a retrieve for my dog.

One of the beaters, who had a dog with him, was standing beside the river discussing the drive with the bottom gun and they were talking about the two dead pheasants that were lying across the river up the other side of the dene. As I approached them, the gun told me that the hen pheasant I had shot was lying about forty metres up the other side, beside a fallen tree, and the cock bird he had shot was twenty metres further up, amongst some small shrubs. The beater was trying hard to get his yellow labrador to cross the river and retrieve both birds. The water was running fairly fast, and was about ten metres

wide, and just over a metre deep. His dog wouldn't have anything to do with it, and the beater tried all he could to get it to cross the river, but had to give up. The labrador didn't seem very keen on water and getting wet.

I said my dog would retrieve the dead pheasants, and by this time several other guns and beaters had joined us. I turned to my dog and said 'Go and find them', and the dog jumped straight into the river, swam across and headed up the side of the dene. I directed him towards the hen pheasant first, and it was then up to the dog to do his job. Within a few minutes, he had found the first bird, and picked it up. He came down the dene to the river with the dead bird in his mouth, jumped straight in and swam across with it. As he came up to me, he sat at my feet with the pheasant in his mouth. I put my hand down, and asked him to release the bird, and he gently released the partly wet bird into my hand.

I then sent the dog out again for the cock pheasant, which was further up the dene. He crossed the river again, and made for where he had picked up the hen bird. I stopped him at this point with the whistle, and sent him further on with hand signals. The dog was working some fifty-odd metres from me, and it was delightful to see him hunting for a bird he hadn't marked. Behind me, the rest of the guns and beaters had gathered to watch me working the animal. The dog was very close to where the pheasant was supposed to have dropped, when it started hunting out to the right. I stopped him again with the whistle, and directed him back to where he was working. A few minutes later he found the cock pheasant and, gently picking it up in his mouth, made straight down the side of the dene to the river, jumped straight into the fast flowing water and came and sat at my feet again, with the partly wet cock pheasant in his mouth.

I am never aware of people when I am working my dog, as my full concentration is on the task in hand. My dog had done a good job, retrieving both shot birds, but I didn't think it was difficult for him, as he was only doing what I had trained him for, although he had also used his own ability. At the end of the day's shooting, one or two of the guns and a few beaters approached me and said how much they had enjoyed watching the dog finding the two birds and retrieving them across the fast-flowing river. This was very rewarding.

9

Dogs in Water

Some dogs like water better than others. Working spaniels, labradors and retrievers in general love it. They seem to take every opportunity to get into water, which both cleans the dogs and cools them down. Many gun dogs will jump straight in, while others will walk around the edge for quite some time and still not venture in, even though they are quite fond of it.

I once had a labrador dog that would not have anything to do with water, no matter how much encouragement I tried to give it. It even tried to avoid getting its feet wet by walking round puddles! I have heard some owners of gun dogs say that they just push or kick their dogs into the water, as they would never otherwise go in on their own account, not even for a wild duck, or a dummy that has been flung in. I don't think you will get very far with a gun dog by doing this. Even if the dog is not very keen, you may still be able, with time and patience, to train and develop it to venture into pools, rivers and streams.

If your dog is keen on retrieving game birds, then this can be used to try to get it into water, although it may take a long time. Remember, if you are trying to get your animal into deep water, do it in the summer time or when the dog is hot. Farm collies are not usually known to be very keen on water, probably for the reason that they are out in all weathers and work amongst long wet grass and

The author with his daughter, Helen, his friend Mike Sharman and springer spaniel, Patch

A pair of springer spaniels from different litters. There are various breeds of springer spaniel gun dog with some breeds being smaller than others

The author with a young springer spaniel at a training session. In a stubble field a training session can last about an hour or so using a dried hare skin dummy or two

A springer spaniel retrieving a training dummy over a stone wall. The dummy is made from a dried hare skin wrapped around a piece of brush handle about 30 cm long. This encourages the dog to pick the dummy up by the middle and not trail it along the ground

Dogs in their kennels with a handmade wire run. The run allows the dogs to see what's going on around them and stops them from getting bored

While the author was on holiday in Scotland his wife Kathleen, daughter Helen, and son Richard, came across this golden retriever gun dog with her young puppies

Game shooters and dogs at the end of a pheasant drive

Kathleen Adair and a friend with their springer spaniels

A shooter with his gundogs before moving out on to the grouse moor. This is a shoot in Cumberland at which the author is a guest from time to time

A gamekeeper checking over the morning's bag of grouse. The grouse are set out to cool before being put into a basket for the dealer

Gamekeepers rebuilding a stone grouse butt on the Durham moors. Very harsh weather with heavy falls of snow and hard frosts can damage the stone grouse butts. Sheep can also damage the butts by climbing on parts of them

A gamekeeper checking the grouse butts before the shooting season starts

heather, so they are often very wet. This keeps them clean, and therefore there is no need for them to go into water. Collies have long hair, and are affected by hot weather, but will normally make for the shade when it is very hot, rather than water.

However, you do get the occasional farm collie that takes readily to water. Often dogs like this are more interested in other things, such as going into water or flushing game birds, than they are in working amongst sheep and cattle. I have known several that were useless at working with animals, for which they were bred, but were very loyal to the farmer and made a good family pet. I have also known certain collie dogs that would follow the farmer's heels all day from getting up in the morning, right through until bedtime. I have also found that a collie dog which was no good at working on the farm was usually a bitch, and was so loyal that the farmer never expected her to work. The dog was basically the farmer's pet – full stop! Often, these are the animals that like water.

I think many collies kept as family pets in the towns and cities never get a chance to clean themselves properly amongst long wet grass and heather. Sometimes they may get wet when out being exercised if it's raining, and this will help to clean their coats to some extent. Some owners wash their dogs on a regular basis, although some kept as pets jump in for a swim at the first opportunity they get, for this cleans and cools them, as well as getting rid of any unwanted parasites which may be clinging to their long coats.

A friend of mine has always kept a collie as a family pet, and the dog has been very well cared for. Its coat is always shining like a new penny, and the dog is taken out for about an hour's exercise and walk every day. It is fed just once a day, and is as fit as a fiddle. My friends live several miles from the seaside, but once a week they make a point of taking the dog there, where it thoroughly enjoys a swim and play in the water. This regular weekly swim is sufficient to keep it clean. The animal lives in the house with the family and is treated as one of them. The dog is very protective of the family, and woe betide anyone that tries to harm them.

When a rough shoot is being worked with gun dogs, the dogs are normally working at full stretch and hunting to flush game birds and ground game for their masters. If you happen to have a springer spaniel, these dogs cover so much ground that their work rate is tremendous. The dogs may have a drink from any water hole or stream which is convenient when they are at a shoot. For instance, I was out with some friends walking a rough shoot one Saturday early in November around the village of Wall in Northumberland. There were three of us with dogs, including myself. When we came to an old railway line a farmer friend of mine, who also has a springer spaniel, suggested that I work one side of the railway track with my dog, and he and his dog would work the other side. The other shooters were lined up in the fields on either side of the disused track, and any birds flushed were left for them to have a shot at.

The railway track, a good mile long, belonged to some of my farmer friends who were shooting with us. One of them had been feeding the pheasants along there, so the dogs had plenty of work to do to flush the birds, as the ground cover was fairly thick. Part of the track was fenced off, and one of the farmers kept a few pigs running on this part of the track all the time. These lived in an old railway carriage, and a water supply was laid on for them, piped into three ground troughs – old stone-glazed kitchen sinks about thirty centimetres deep, which were ideal for the job.

By the time my friend and I had worked along the track to where the pigs were kept, the springers were puffing and panting, for it was a fairly warm sunny day, despite being late in the year. When we approached the troughs, both animals jumped straight in. They sat there, and kept turning round and round in the water to cool themselves down, drinking at the same time.

To return to training young gun dogs to go into water, remember that this can take a long time, and, like all training, should never be rushed. The best time of year to begin is during the summer months when the weather is warmer. It is no good just pushing the dog into the water if it is not very keen, but most breeds will go in if the conditions are right at the time.

Take, for instance, a young 1-year-old labrador dog that is being trained as a gun dog but shows an aversion to entering water. It will be much more useful if it will retrieve ducks or dead game birds that happen to fall into a fast-flowing river. If the dog enjoys retrieving game birds, sticks, or has a favourite toy, then use something like this to encourage it. If the dog is being trained for work, put it through a training session before you approach the water with it. First of all, pick a warm day, and start with a small, shallow pond or stream with some deep pools. Let the dog play around for quite a while until it is hot and panting, or is warm from the training session, then take it to the edge of the water. At this stage, use something the dog enjoys playing with, for example a training dummy or a stick, as game birds will be out of season at this time of year. First of all, make the dog sit beside you, then throw his favourite stick beside the shallow water, and get the animal to retrieve it. Do this a few times when the dog is hot. The next stage is then to throw the stick into the shallow water, and get the dog to retrieve it. Two or three retrieves from shallow water at this stage is sufficient.

When the dog has begun going into shallow water, at another training session gradually begin putting the stick into deeper water until it has to swim to retrieve it. This may take from as little as one week, to as long as six – but don't rush it; take your time, for this is how you are most likely to succeed. Remember to have the dog warmed up before trying it in the water. I have had to spend hours and hours with some young gun dogs to try to get them in! The dogs have to be in the correct frame of mind at the time, and the conditions have to be right to do this, although some gun dogs will do it as long as there is something in the water for them to retrieve. You can't expect them all to just jump straight into a deep cold river or pond from a warm car, or into a cold stream on a freezing cold winter's day. If you think about it, would you like to jump into a cold bath in a cold bathroom? The thought of it sends shivers up my spine. It is also possible to use an experienced gun dog that is fond of water to help train a young dog that is unused, or averse, to it. Again, start in the summer, when the weather and water temperatures are much higher, and always begin in shallow water. I can remember a young yellow labrador I once had, that wouldn't go into water at any price. It was really no good as a gun dog, but made a lovely family pet. I tried various

ways to get this animal into water but failed; the dog just didn't like it! This is the only dog I have ever had that was averse to water – in fact, it was very reluctant to go out on a wet day. I had another two trained labradors at the time, and I used both of these to try to help the young dog into the water. When the animal was a year old, it was the middle of summer, and I spent many nights with all three dogs beside the river, or the duck pond. The young dog would run along the river bank, barking at the other two swimming in the river, but it wouldn't join them.

I tried him in very shallow water first, where the water only covered his toes, but still he showed no interest. I also tried taking him to the seaside several times. I knew he was going to be no good as a gun dog as I had made many attempts trying to get him into water on his training sessions. He just wasn't up to what was required of him, or it may have been my fault for not being able to train such an animal. The dogs that I train as gun dogs must have some ability before I can train them to a reasonable standard. However, I do get the odd dud one, and this young labrador dog was certainly one. He did turn out to be a good family pet, though, and was very good-natured and welcomed everyone to our house.

Keeping dogs as clean family pets can be quite a problem. Some people bath and shampoo them. But if too much soapy material is used, it will be inclined to remove some of the natural oil from the dog's coat. All breeds of dog can have a 'doggy' smell, and if you keep them in the house, this smell can sometimes be unpleasant if some action is not taken to overcome the problem. I know when my dogs need washing, and so does my wife, but when you have animals around you all the time, you can get used to the smell of them, and then it's only other people that notice this when they visit your home. Some people spray their dogs with perfume regularly to give them a nice scent!

Although we are a nation of animal lovers, we are not very good at taking our dogs out for a walk when it's raining, or when it's windy and wet. But these are good conditions for exercising them, as they will clean themselves where there is long wet grass or water. Put on some waterproof clothes and go out for a hike for an hour or so each day before or after your evening meal; it will do you both the world of good! If it is very windy and wet, try to plan your walk so that you have your back to the wind all the time, as this will also stop the rain blowing into your face. Or take the dog into a wood, where you will be sheltered from the wind, and the dog can get cleaned in long wet grass or bracken. The heavier the rain, the better it is, as it will clean the animal, especially if it has a long coat. This is far better than shampooing or bathing it.

When it is snowing heavily, this will also keep the dog clean. You may find it will roll in the snow from time to time, and this helps because the snow sticks to, or wipes against its coat. In general, dogs know what they need as far as cleaning themselves is concerned. We humans think we know what is best for them, but we don't, for the dogs know better than us. If they are given the space, and have continual contact with the soil, they will look after themselves better than we humans can look after them.

I try to take my dog out for an hour's walk or work out each day if possible, no matter what the weather is like. I vary the route depending a great deal on the weather and time of day. I also try to get him washed or cleaned at least once a fortnight; there are certain small rivers and pools where he likes to swim if we happen to be in that area. If the weather is very dry, then I normally arrange it that we end the walk or work-out beside the water, where the dog will have a swim and clean and cool himself down.

Some dogs smell more than others, and my springer spaniel will start to smell 'doggy' after a fortnight if his coat hasn't been wet or cleaned. Last year, for instance, we put the dog into our local kennels for about ten days while we were on holiday. These kennels are very clean and very well managed and run, and the owners look after my dog very well indeed. However, when we went to pick up the dog, he still smelt doggy. The reason was that he hadn't been able to clean his coat in the rain or long grass. I soon had him in the water that evening, and he was very pleased to get in for a swim and to clean himself. Interestingly, that evening he went straight into the water without being told, and he knew where we were going, long before we ever got there! Dogs are more intelligent than we give them credit for. My dog's looks and body language when we entered the car that evening told me he wanted to be in water.

This 'doggy' smell doesn't really matter very much if the dog is kept in kennels, or if it has a run to play out in, as it will automatically get cleaned when it's raining.

During the winter months, when the weather is cold and frosty, a dog will usually have to be hot and bothered before jumping into cool water to clean itself, unless sent in to retrieve a dead duck or a shot game bird which has dropped there. But, if your dog is standing at the back door or in the garden when it's bucketing down with rain, don't call it into the house. You will find that, though it knows it can get under cover, it may prefer to stay out in the rain to get its coat clean. Never think you always know best in this respect. Some of our farm collies with long coats liked nothing better than standing out in the open yard when it was pouring with rain, even though they had plenty of open sheds to shelter in if they wished. My mother used to feel sorry for them, but the dogs knew what they wanted and what they needed. I often used to stand in the farm house and watch the collie dogs standing with their backs to the rain if it was blowing, for this was one of their methods of cleaning themselves.

We humans poison our dogs by overfeeding them. Sometimes, you will see your dog eating grass, which means that the animal is lacking in some sort of mineral or medicine. Let it eat as much grass as it wants to; it will know when it has eaten what it needs, and, left alone, the dog will sort itself out without human interference. Dogs are not the only animals to do this, for sometimes cattle in a bare pasture will persistently lick the soil to get the minerals they need.

10

Following Wounded Game

Right from when I was a small boy my father used to drum into me that wounded game must be tracked down and collected at the time the bird or animal is shot and wounded – not the next day, or when the gamekeeper or dog-handler has time. And this must be done even if it means spoiling some of the day's shooting. When visiting various game shoots with him I soon learned what this really meant. I came across, and was taught the trade and shooting etiquette by, a number of true country sportsmen. So it was my father, landowners and game-keepers who tutored me in the elements of the sport of shooting and working with gun dogs.

It sometimes saddens me a bit, when I am out with a shooting party today, if a wounded game bird can't be found quickly, and someone suggests that we move on, because the gamekeeper can look for the wounded bird later. None of my regular shooting friends would do this – at least one dog man would drop back and hunt for the injured bird until it was found. In most cases, it will be somebody paying a lot of money for the privilege of shooting game birds that wants to press on. The thought of losing some shooting for the sake of hunting for a wounded bird, and holding up their sport, is not to be considered.

There are people from all walks of life shooting game birds today, and some of them pay a lot of money for the privilege of the sport, but don't have a clue how the countryside ticks. Some visit the country just when it's the shooting season, and then only to kill as many game birds as possible in a day, for which they are paying.

To hunt for, and find most wounded game, be it fur or feather, you need to have a good gun dog or gun dogs, because many injured birds and animals may travel a long distance before they find a place to hide and die. Sometimes, an injured bird will find the most unusual place to hide, and that may be up a drainpipe, under some outbuildings, along a river bank, or under some tree roots.

I have hunted and tracked down wounded game birds and animals with dogs in both Scotland and England, and on all the various types of shoot, since I started shooting as a young boy. Some were easy to find, whilst others took several hours to locate, with a great deal depending on the weather conditions, how strong or weak the bird or animal's scent was and how much start the injured game had on the dog.

You may ask, 'Why do sportsmen not shoot to kill the game dead in the first place, rather than wound it?' The art is indeed to kill all game dead quickly and cleanly with the first shot, and that is what all sportsmen set out to do. But there is always the odd game bird or ground game that gets wounded. There is only a very, very small percentage of game shot each season that is wounded, and an extremely small minority that are not found and collected. Nevertheless, for a sportsman, it's the odd one that is one too many. Many gamekeepers and dog-handlers who get the job of picking up wounded birds at a shoot may hunt their dogs well into the darkness to find injured game, and some will even go out the next day to search again if they think it has not been accounted for.

There are two main reasons why I think a few game birds are wounded, rather than killed outright. Firstly, shots are often fired at birds that are out of range. Many shooters just can't seem to judge the distance between them and the birds, and they think they may just have a chance of bringing the bird down. However, all they do is wound it, and one pellet is enough to injure any bird hit in the right place. Another reason for wounded birds can be that the gun doesn't fit the shooter, who is then likely to wound more birds than he kills cleanly (he may blame the cartridges for this). I have a sixteen-bore sidelock ejector shotgun that I bought second-hand, and when I first went shooting with it I was shooting low, wounding or missing most of what I aimed at. I soon had the gun looked at and altered to fit me. There was too much bend on the stock, so I had it straightened a bit, which lifted the gun barrels up, and this improved my aim.

Ground game, such as hares, are sometimes wounded in the hindquarters, because the shooter is normally firing from behind the animal. An injured hare can travel a long way before it finally stops, the distance depending a great deal on how seriously it has been wounded. Last year I was out with a party on a rough shoot, part of which was a fairly large grouse moor, and six of us were walking in line across the rough ground on the edge of the moor. The gun on my left fired at a hare that ran across in front of us and wounded it in the hind legs. I noted that it was injured, and thought it wouldn't travel very far before it dropped dead. How wrong I was! The person that shot it, who had no gun dog with him, walked across to where he had wounded the animal, while the rest of us strolled on in line across the rough ground. As we walked further away from our companion, we noticed he couldn't find his shot game. One of the other shooters said that he hadn't shot the hare in the first place, but I knew better, as I had seen it being shot and wounded. The gamekeeper came across to me and said, 'Hunter, go and try to find the hare with your dog'. I quickly dropped back to where I saw the wounded animal, and discussed its whereabouts with the chap who had shot it. He was pretty sure it was hard hit, and wouldn't travel very far. I soon had the dog hunting around the area, and it quickly picked up the scent and started to follow it. I kept it close at hand, but encouraged the dog to find the wounded animal. In a very short time the dog and I were half a mile or so away out on the moor, still tracking the hare from where it had been shot. (You should never let your dog go on its own to hunt a wounded hare in such open country, no matter how experienced it is, because it could end up in the next county and get lost.) The dog was hunting for the animal along a gully about fifteen metres in front of me, and the scent of the hare was getting very strong, so I knew that the animal wasn't very far ahead. Sure enough, twenty metres or so further on, there was the hare, lying dead beside some rocks. The dog and I had tracked it for nearly three-quarters of a mile before we found it!

Ground game that are wounded and run on, are usually called runners. Game birds that are wounded are also termed runners if they hit the ground, then run on but can't fly.

Funny, nobody knows your gun dog like you yourself. This was highlighted at a recent pheasant shoot where I was a guest and one of the standing guns. There was a gun on my right and one on my left, and I was standing on an old farm track, with the dog at my heel. I had just got into position, when a cock pheasant came flying high and fast over my head. I swung the gun onto the bird, and fired. The pheasant veered off to my left, and dropped into the field opposite. As soon as it hit the ground it was on its feet, running away from us fast, as I had only winged the bird, which I hate to do. I sent the dog out to where it had first dropped and, at the same time, several more pheasants were coming over the guns. I kept my eye on the animal as it was hunting around for the bird. During a break, when no pheasants were coming over us, one of the other standing guns called across to me, and asked if he should go and look for the wounded bird. At the same time, the gun on my other side also asked if he could help. I was pretty annoyed with their remarks, and replied politely that this was the dog's job. I turned to the dog again as it was still hunting around the area where the bird had come down. I spoke very sharply to it, and instructed it to go find the bird, and stop messing around. By this time, the wounded pheasant was well away, as five minutes or so had passed. I turned again to the shooting, as the beaters were calling, and pheasants were being flushed forward. I shot one or two more on this drive, which dropped around us. The beaters by this time had arrived beside the guns, and the drive had finished, when we all just happened to turn round, and there was my dog coming up the farm lane with the cock pheasant in his mouth. What a beautiful sight it was, to see him returning with the bird, as he must have been gone ten minutes or so to find the runner. The two shooters who had called to me earlier to ask if they should help find the wounded bird, came over to me at the end of the drive and said that they never thought the dog would find this runner. They didn't know the capability of my animal. To me, this was just another job which the dog had done very well.

Sometimes a wounded pheasant will go so far up a field drain or a water cundy that the puzzle is how to get it out! (A cundy is an old stone drain, which may channel water from the highway or from an old stone quarry; sometimes they are beside railway embankments and river banks.) If the dog can't get into it to retrieve the wounded bird, because the entrance is too small, then sometimes it is necessary to try different means to reach it. One might end up having to dig out the bird, or even pull it out. A walking stick can be useful here, for sometimes one can hook the bird and drag it to where one can get hold of it with the hands. Wounded birds run into these peculiar

A wild hen pheasant sitting on nine eggs. Some pheasants lay their eggs in places where sheep and cattle can easily trample on them. This nest was beside one of the author's cattle sheds and the chicks were all hatched and reared

The beaters at a pheasant shoot waiting to start the drive. These are mainly young people out to make a bit of pocket money. The amounts vary from between £20 and £40 for a day's beating and there may be a lump of cheese and a beer thrown in at lunch time

The gamekeeper collecting the shot pheasants at the end of a drive

A springer spaniel retrieving a cock pheasant. Note how the dog has tried to pick up the pheasant by the middle

A friend of the author with his dogs which he works at various shoots

A black labrador finds and retrieves a pheasant. The dog was very gentle with the bird as it returned it to its master

A pointer dog at work on top of a stone wall. This pointer dog waited until it was told to move in and flush the game. To get some pointers and setters to flush the game you can give the signal by shuffling one foot in the grass or the heather

Game shooters near the Scottish border having a chat at the end of a pheasant drive

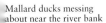
Mallard ducks messing about near the river bank

The author sent his dog into the pond to retrieve a mallard duck he had shot

Note how the dog has tried to pick the duck up by the middle to stop it trailing along the ground

This woman loves her dogs. She always has border terrier dogs and the odd setter

places because of fear, and in general they never go very far into drains, as they always like to see daylight. It is not very often that I find a wounded bird has gone to ground and I can't get it out.

Wild duck such as mallard, can sometimes take a lot of finding when they get wounded. When I am shooting at my duck pond at dusk, the occasional wounded duck can sometimes tuck itself underneath a tussock of rushes, or even travel a long distance on the ground from the pond, before deciding to stop and hide. I can well remember one night when I was shooting ducks with some friends at my father's pond in Ayrshire, Scotland. I shot at the first duck that came into the pond, and it dropped on the ground beside the water a few metres away from my dog and me. Because it was dusk, I didn't see it fall; I just heard the thud as it hit the ground. I had a yellow labrador at the time, and I didn't send it to retrieve the bird as I thought there might be some more ducks coming into the pond at the time.

This was the only duck I shot that night, and when we finished shooting, I thought I had nothing to do but to send my dog to pick up and retrieve the dead bird. But it turned out somewhat differently! My dog kept hunting around for it, as did my friends' dogs, and nothing was to be found. My companions started to tease me, and said I was only dreaming, and had just imagined I had shot the duck to impress them. (They were only joking, for they, too, had heard the duck fall.) We spent half an hour and more hunting for this bird, and still couldn't find it. By this time it was pitch dark, and I first thought that a fox might have moved in and picked up the duck whilst we were standing around the pond waiting for other mallard to come flying in. I had once seen a fox come and pick up a dead pheasant when I was shooting in a wood, and the cheeky animal was only a few metres away from me when he picked it up!

The next morning, I went back to the duck pond at about nine o'clock, and my dog and I started hunting again to try to find the bird. The labrador soon picked up some scent, and I encouraged him on. He quickly moved away from the pond, over a small marsh, and onto the old railway track, and there, amongst some nettles and wood, he retrieved the duck, still alive, and shot in the wing. It was some two hundred metres away from where I had shot it at the pond. The weather had started to freeze the night I hit it, and by the time we started to look for it, the ground had a crust on, and the scent of the bird had partly disappeared. However, the next morning my dog had managed to pick up the duck's scent, although it took it an hour or so to do so, and he did a good job in finding this wounded bird.

Sometimes, certain events stick in one's mind. One of these occurred last year when I was at a pheasant shoot. It was very wet, with hail and sleet showers, and windy and cold as well. Wise men would never think of shooting in such conditions, but the friends I was out with wouldn't let the weather stop them. We had shot a few pheasants during the morning drives, but after lunch, even though the weather seemed to be deteriorating, we still carried on. In the afternoon I shot at a pheasant that came flying fast down the wood. I hit it, though not very hard, and brought it down, but the bird no sooner hit the ground than it picked itself up and ran off up into the wood opposite.

I would normally leave this runner for the dog men, but, because of the horrible weather, I thought I would give my dog something to do, rather than keep it sitting beside me cold, wet and miserable. I never thought a wounded bird would be so difficult to track down and find! It had crossed a stream, run through a copse, and was picked up in the wood where it was reared, still alive, about three hundred metres or so away from where I shot it. Experience plays a great part in tracking down a wounded pheasant like this one, and you have to know your dog to let it use its wisdom and talents. Again I knew my animal, and if this wounded bird was on the ground, my dog would pick it up.

The occasional wounded bird or hare just can't be found and retrieved, and this saddens me very much, especially if I am one of the dog men at a shoot, picking up dead or wounded birds and hares behind the guns. Thankfully, this does not happen very often, as my dog and I will work and hunt for a wounded bird or animal until it is pitch black. This was the training I received from my father, and which I will never forget.

A small party of us were walking a rough shoot one particularly windy day when it was really blowing a gale, although it was dry. We could find some shelter in the woods and coverts, or would try to walk on the lee side of the land. It was so windy that I couldn't talk to the nearest gun walking in line with me, which meant I had to look and watch where I was shooting for safety's sake, and the other guns had to do the same. We had just climbed over a stone wall into a fairly large conifer plantation that was reasonably open, with some good ground cover, and, because of the type of day it was, I thought this would be a good place for a few pheasants to be hiding out of the strong wind.

We had just lined up in the coppice and started walking through, when a cock pheasant was flushed by one of the gun dogs at the other end of the line from me. I was the outside gun walking along the edge of the wood on the right. The pheasant lifted and flew forward, and at the same time the wind caught the bird, and it was really travelling! The gun on my left had two shots at it; I could see it falling and thought it was dead. The pheasant, however, had landed on its feet, and it immediately took off, running like fury away from us; the bird was certainly hit, but couldn't fly. It made for the edge of the wood in front of me, and started running along the bottom of the stone wall inside the coppice. We carried on walking through the wood, and I thought that by the time we reached the end of it, two or three hundred metres on, my dog would have picked up the wounded bird. There was plenty of ground cover like bracken and long grass all the way along the base of the wall, for the pheasant to hide amongst. My dog kept following the scent of the wounded bird right to the end of the wood, but there was no sign of the pheasant.

The wind was blowing behind us, which had caught the pheasant as it lifted, and made it such a difficult shot. At the end of the wood we all gathered in the corner to discuss where this wounded bird could be. My dog and I were given the job of trying to find it, while the rest of the shooters went on. I thought to myself that the dog hadn't found it in the wood, and I wondered if I would ever be able to do so now, fifteen to twenty minutes later. Also, because it was so windy and dry, the scent of the bird wasn't very good (I can always tell by the way my dog is working how good the conditions are for scenting a wounded bird or animal, and very windy weather does impair the scent).

On the outside of the plantation, there were several acres of rough land which contained whin bushes, bracken and gorse bushes. The dog hunted this rough ground for over an hour, and found nothing, though he had picked up various scents which I thought might have been the wounded bird. We backtracked into the wood we had come from to try to pick up the scent, but the dog just couldn't get onto it. I spent the rest of that day with my dog hunting for this wounded pheasant, but had to give in as darkness fell. I am always very sorry when the day ends like this, but as I have said before, there is always the occasional wounded bird or animal that can't be found and picked up.

11

Ailments and Injuries

There is nothing worse than having a gun dog out of condition for any length of time, or injured right in the middle of the shooting season, when the pheasants are in full swing. I have known some shooters who have not turned up to a shoot because their dogs were lame or sick. Gun dogs, like humans, do fall ill, and can be out of condition when the shooting season starts, and when they are most needed.

When you have a good working gun dog you will always get more shooting than a chap who hasn't got a dog, especially on a rough shoot. Gamekeepers from far and wide are always willing to use dog men to beat for them at their shoots. A well-trained animal is part of the field equipment; some dog-owners only get invited to various shoots to beat because they have good gun dogs. A man with a dog, beating at a fairly large pheasant shoot, is likely to get about £25 for a day's work. And the beaters may also get a can or two of beer and a bit of lunch, such as a meat pie or two, or a lump of cheese.

Gun dogs, like any other creatures on this earth, will perform much better when they are fully fit and in good condition. Like humans, they can have their off days too. Sometimes, a good dog will work with little instruction, as it knows exactly what its handler requires of it and will partly be reading its owner's mind. A good gun dog hunting out in front should keep looking back from time to time, checking its position and direction. This is when a gun dog is most delightful to watch, quartering the ground at full stretch, covering all the undergrowth with its nose, and not missing any fur or feather which may be lying tight beneath the ground cover; a well-trained and fit dog will see the job is done well in order to please its master. But dogs thrashing through brambles and bracken do get a few scrapes and scratches from time to time as they search through the rough cover for game birds. Working gun dogs are more likely to incur injuries than dogs that are kept as pets. The most common ones are cuts, sprains and eye and ear damage, caused by hunting through rough woods containing brambles, thorns and barbed wire. And in various corners of woodland there may be a danger of broken glass bottles and empty open tin cans, which can cut a dog's pad and keep the animal from working for a few weeks until it heals.

RICKETS

Many ailments from which working dogs and farm collies used to suffer have almost disappeared. Rickets was mainly caused by the dogs not being fed a proper balanced diet. Many were fed only on scraps of food, and some were often given just bread and water, or boiled maize and water. Many young dogs were often fed large quantities of scrap foods at a time, these containing little meat protein, which is good for young and adult dogs, when what they needed was small meals with all the essential nutrients two or three times a day after weaning then later one meal per day. Many beef farmers and game-keepers used to keep a house cow, and some of their dogs were fed milk in their diet. This is a natural food and is a staple diet for any young animal.

It was thought by some dog-breeders that rickets was also caused by damp and cold beds, and lack of regular exercise. However, this is not so; these things are more likely to cause rheumatics in dogs, but rickets is due to a Vitamin D deficiency, as well as lack of sunlight. Rickets is heard of very little today, because there is now a good variety of tinned and bagged dog foods on the market, as well as many well-balanced dog meals and biscuits available.

DISTEMPER

Distemper has always been a problem amongst our canine friends, cropping up from time to time, especially in urban areas, although there are some good vaccines available today which are very effective. Many young dogs which get the virus and haven't been vaccinated may only have a fifty per cent chance of survival, as there is effectively no cure for it. A few years ago, a number of dogs in the area where I live in the north died in an outbreak of distemper, which worried the veterinary surgeons and many dog-owners. It had been a long time since it had presented such a problem in the district, and this outbreak seemed to start in a village some fifteen miles away from my home.

Distemper is not often seen these days, because in general people vaccinate their dogs regularly. But once they stop doing this, the disease returns, and this is what seems to have happened in our district, for it was during the winter months, an unusual time for the virus to strike. About twenty dogs were treated during the outbreak, and approximately half of them died of it. If a dog has not

been in contact with the virus, or with other dogs that have it, and is not running a temperature, then it is not too late to have it vaccinated.

Some outbreaks of distemper can be particularly severe, and usually end with the dogs showing nervous symptoms, which often end in death. It is very easily transmitted, even via humans, and the most obvious symptoms in dogs are the signs of a cold, with red runny eyes, and a runny nose.

ARTHRITIS

Arthritis in dogs is thought to appear with old age, but this is not always the case. I once had a young gun dog that fell down an embankment and injured his back. Although he was treated by the vet and rested for a long time, he was never right after this accident and within a year had developed arthritis in the back. This was a sharp, intelligent young dog and had the makings of a top-quality working gun dog. Eventually I had the dog destroyed for his own good. I was giving him pain-killers in his food every day, but he found it difficult walking after the accident. He was only three years old at the time.

I also had a yellow labrador that one summer's evening was hit fairly hard by a car on the hindquarters and keeled over. He wasn't in the habit of straying onto the road – he would usually just be around the garden – but that fateful evening he just happened to wander out. It was an unusual thing for him to do, and he paid for it. He was pretty sore around the back legs for quite a while, but, as it was the close season, there was plenty of time for him to recover before shooting started again. However, things didn't work out like that. The vet looked over the dog at the time of the accident, thought he would take several months to recover, and so left me a supply of pain-killing tablets. But the dog never really recovered from this accident. He would be walking along, then all of a sudden his hind legs would give way, and he would fall down in severe pain. He also developed a type of limp when walking. Arthritis soon set into his hindquarter joints, which got worse. Although I kept the dog for a while after this accident, he never worked again. I managed to keep him from suffering any pain, but after a while, the dog started trailing his hind legs, and eventually I had him put down. He was only four-and-a-half years old and coming into his prime. Despite developing arthritis after the car accident, he never lost his instinct to hunt and flush game birds, and I often had to stop him doing this.

EYE TROUBLES

Eye troubles in gun dogs can be a real nuisance. If a dog's eye gets pricked by a sharp thorn from bushes or shrubs as it works through them, it may return home from a day's work in the field with a red, inflamed eye. This inflammation may last a few days if not treated. It will probably heal itself anyway, but there are some very good sterile eye drops and lotions on the market today, which you can obtain from the vet, that will relieve symptoms resulting from infections and minor injuries of this sort and help the dog's recovery.

However, if a gun dog returns from the field with a serious eye injury – if it has a deep cut in the eye, say or its eye is completely closed and swollen due to the damage received – then waste no time in getting your dog to the vet.

EARS

Certain breeds of gun dog, such as spaniels, are well known for having trouble with their ears. Not all long-eared breeds suffer this way, and setters and retrievers, which are much bigger dogs, although they also have large ears, don't have this problem as much as spaniels. The reason that spaniels are prone to this problem I think is because they have shorter legs, and are more inclined to get drops of water and other bits of rubbish in their ears as they hunt through long wet grass, small shrubs and woods. When the dogs are hunting and quartering the ground at speed, their ears can flop over if they turn quickly, exposing them to foreign bodies. I can almost always tell when my spaniel will have an ear infection. If I am working it for a few wet days on the trot at pheasant shoots or on a rough shoot, I can be pretty sure that I shall have to treat the dog's ears within a fortnight or so afterwards. I don't usually get much trouble with ears during the summer months, though, because my dogs are not working amongst long wet grass and shrubs.

It is unwise to stuff a dog's ears with powders or creams

without getting advice from the vet first. All dogs have wax glands in their ears, which produce a wax that keeps the inside of the animal's ears clean. Nothing should be put into the ears which will interfere with this process.

There are various infections which dogs develop that need different treatments. I usually put a few drops of an ear lotion into my animal's ears two or three times a week, which soon clears up the infection caused by picking up foreign bodies during hunting. Check with the vet if you are having problems with your dog, for I am sure he or she will provide you with the right advice and treatment.

WOUNDS

Although the larger varieties of gun dog are not so prone to ear problems, they do all share similar problems which occur when working them in the field amongst game birds. Wounds can keep a gun dog out of action for weeks if they are not attended to properly and efficiently. Depending a great deal on how deep the injury is, and where it is sited, one will quickly have to decide what action to take. If the dog needs to see a vet, then get it attended to straight away; don't wait, thinking it may heal itself, for it may not. For instance, all deep wounds which need stitching have to be sewn up within two or three hours if they are to knit together properly. It is no use thinking that tomorrow will do, because it is more convenient for you to take the dog along to the vet then.

If you want your dog to recover quickly, attend to it immediately, even if it means leaving a shoot mid-morning.

At one time some gamekeepers were able to sew up a gun dog that got seriously wounded. The dog would be muzzled first, then the wound would be washed with a weak solution of antiseptic before being sewn up with a surgical needle and horsehair or stout fishing gut. I can well remember my father attending to all our dogs' wounds. If one of our animals was seriously cut when out working in the field at a pheasant shoot, my father would pack up straight away and come home to attend to it. If the dog's injury was serious, my father would leave just after the first pheasant drive.

Not all cuts in dogs need to be stitched. A tight bandage tied on for a few days, then changed, may be satisfactory for healing many small cuts and bruises, provided the wound is cleaned properly before it is first bandaged. My father was very particular about the health and care of his gun dogs. When one of his dogs was bandaged up, he used to keep a muzzle on it all the time to prevent it from tearing open the wound. This was only removed when the animal was being fed and watered.

You may be out somewhere with a shooting party, and your dog gets a leg deeply gashed or cut on barbed wire, and the wound needs to be sewn up. However, due to the circumstances, you can't get the dog to the vet until the evening. What can you do about it yourself? First of all, find something you can use to bandage the animal's wound tightly, such as a clean handkerchief, a scarf or, alternatively, a tie which someone at the shoot is most likely to be wearing. Use it to bind round the injury until you get the dog home to see the vet. The most important thing is to stop the dog from working any more that day. It would also be wise to keep it with you, for, if you shut it up in a shed or in the car until you have finished shooting, you will probably find that the bandaging has been torn off, and the wound may have been infected with dirt, which will delay the healing time, keeping the dog off his work for even longer.

Gun dogs get all sorts of injuries when out working in the field. I can remember a labrador I once had which was sent to retrieve a hare that I had shot in the next field. On the way he had to go through a wire fence made up of several strands of plain wire, with a strand of barbed wire on the top. Somehow, as the dog was jumping through the plain wires, his right front leg got caught between them, and the strands twisted, trapping the dog's leg. The harder it pulled to get free, the more the wires tightened, causing it a lot of pain. As two or three shooters and I approached the trapped animal, he was showing his teeth in great distress. One of them, who knew the dog well, went over to the fence to free him when I stopped him. I said the dog would bite him, so just leave it.

There was an elderly gentleman at the shoot who had a war wound in one leg. Along with his gun, he always carried a shooting stick with a leather handle and seat, and he used to sit on it when he wasn't walking in order to save his bad leg. I asked him if I could borrow his stick for a minute and then walked over to my trapped dog, pushed the handle of the shooting stick into the dog's mouth, and let him bite hard on it while one of the other shooters freed his leg. The dog's limb wasn't badly damaged, only a little bit bruised, and nothing appeared broken. The accident steadied him down for the rest of the shoot, and he limped around for the next few days, but within a fortnight, he was out shooting again and had forgotten the whole thing.

To stop a dog tearing a bandage off an injured leg or paw, cut the bottom out of a small plastic bucket, and put the dog's head through the hole in the bucket bottom, and tie it behind the dog's front legs and shoulders. The bucket should be removed to feed and water the animal. You could also muzzle it, for this would also stop it from tearing and pulling at the bandage.

WORMS

Worms have always been a problem with dogs, as they are also with other animals, such as sheep and cattle. All young dogs and puppies should be wormed at an early age, anything from seven weeks onwards as the puppies may be infested with worms from their mother.

Working gun dogs are likely to pick up worm larvae when they are hunting in fields and meadows where sheep and cattle graze. The dogs may need to be wormed at regular intervals. It is difficult to say how often, but maybe once a year. My dogs are wormed about every six months or so, because they are always in the fields on our farm, either for exercise or for training. During the shooting season, my dogs are working nearly every other day on different land, where there are both sheep and cattle. There are many signs when dogs need worming. Their coats may go dull, and sometimes they rub their bottoms along the ground.

ANAL GLANDS

The glands in a dog's bottom sometimes get blocked, with the result that they give off a sweet smell. Many breeds of dog and cat get this problem. You may also see the dog licking its bottom and rubbing it along the ground. When this happens, I normally clean out my dog's blocked anal glands myself. It is, however, better to take your animal along to the vet to get them to do it for you; the glands may have become infected, so the dog may need some antibiotics to clear up the problem. If your dog has a tendency to this trouble, you can do something about it yourself, though. First of all, it may be getting too much protein in its food and drink, for example too much milk. Also, give your dog some roughage in its food, like bran, and give it a bone to chew from time to time, for this will help.

DIABETES

Some dogs are so inbred that they inherit defects from their parents, and sometimes the faults are not discovered until the dog starts to work. I have a spaniel at the moment that came from a breeder who is known for producing good-quality working gun dogs. I selected and bought this pedigree puppy, and he looked and seemed sound at the time. I started to train him when he was ten weeks old, as I usually do.

When the young dog was about fifteen months old, I was having a training session with him when suddenly he looked at me and keeled over, having a fit which lasted for about five minutes or so. He was finished for doing any more training that day. My first thoughts were to wonder if the dog was having an epileptic fit, or whether he was just exhausted from his training session. Several months later the same thing happened again. The young dog keeled over when I was working with him in a small wood.

I promptly had the problem investigated. It was occurring when the dog had been working at full stretch for an hour or so, at a training session or flushing pheasants. It transpired that the dog's pancreas wasn't making enough sugar to keep him charging on and working hard for much of the day, so he just keeled over and had a fit. I was advised by the vet to try to get some sugar into him before we set off shooting in the morning. I always carry a Mars bar or two along with me when I am going shooting, and I sometimes give one of my dogs a little bit if the dog is really working its heart out at a pheasant shoot and I think that it is tiring a bit. (Carrying a Mars bar along with me goes back to when I was a young boy, a very long time ago. My father used to go to the cattle market every Tuesday to buy or sell cattle from the farm, and rather than have lunch in the cattle market canteen, he bought a couple of Mars bars which would keep him going until he got home at tea time. This is how I started the practice which I have continued ever since. I know some sportsmen with working gun dogs who give their dogs a Mars bar or two when they are out working their animals at game shoots. This is usually done at lunch time, to help keep the dogs fresh for working in the afternoon. I overcame the sugar problem with my dog, by feeding him in the morning before we set off to go game shooting. I also offer him some Mars bars before we leave home. This dog loves chocolate! He may eat three or four large bars in the morning, after being fed and before we go shooting. I know then that the dog will have enough sugar to keep him hunting all day long without keeling over. The most interesting thing is that he will eat only enough Mars bars to provide the amount of sugar he needs. When we are out shooting I often test the dog about lunchtime, to see if he needs any more sugar by offering him a piece or a whole Mars bar. He will sometimes eat half a bar at lunch time, just to top up his sugar levels. Later on in the afternoon, I may offer him another piece. It is most unlikely that he will eat any more chocolate that day. He may sniff it, but he refuses it!

I am now confident that the amount of chocolate he takes in the morning will provide him with sufficient sugar to keep hunting all day without keeling over. This is a marvellous gun dog, and for a dog to tell me just what he needs to work hard all day just shows how intelligent he is. Vets don't know how much sugar he needs when he is working at full stretch all day, flushing pheasants, and I don't either, but the dog knows what his body needs. It provides him with energy quickly. I often give him a bit of chocolate during the day when he is not working!

In 1727, when the cattle drovers were bringing cattle from Falkirk in Scotland to Doncaster in England, nearly two hundred and fifty miles away, some drovers took the boat back home up the east coast, and their dogs had to walk home.

A little girl from Berwick was one day playing outside her house, when two dogs went past. She asked her father if someone had lost his dogs. 'No, no,' was her father's reply, 'These are the drovers' dogs, coming home from Doncaster'. It just shows how clever the dogs were, to find their own way home, when it was such a long distance!